WASHINGTON

—IN—

THE LAP OF ROME

Justin D. Fulton

Bibliographic Information

Washington In the Lap of Rome was originally published in 1888 in Boston by W. KELLAWAY (Office of the Free Press) Tremont Temple.

(Spelling, grammar, and punctuation from the originally published edition has been retained.)

an Ichthus Publications edition

Copyright © 2014 Ichthus Publications
ISBN 10: 1502350629
ISBN 13: 978-1502350626

www.ichthuspublications.com

"WHEREFORE TAKE UNTO YOU THE WHOLE ARMOR OF GOD THAT YE MAY BE ABLE TO WITHSTAND IN THE EVIL DAY, AND HAVING DONE ALL TO STAND."—PAUL.

CONTENTS

PREFACE

"WASHINGTON in the Lap of Rome" has been written to call the attention of the American people to the great trust which has been betrayed, and to the great work which devolves upon them. It uncovers facts which will bring the blush of shame to the cheek of the real Republican and fill his soul with indignation. Fifteen thousand department clerks are under the surveillance of Rome. If it be not true, as is charged, that a private wire runs from the White House, in Washington, to the Cardinal's Palace, in Baltimore, and that every important question touching the interests of Romanism in America is placed before his eye, before it becomes a public act, it *is* true that the Cardinal is a factor in politics. Romanism is the dominant power in the Capitol of the United States. Lincoln, Grant, and Arthur withstood it, and suffered the consequences. The power is unseen. It is shadowy. It inhabits the air and infects it. Romanism is the malaria of the spiritual world. It stupefies the brain, deadens the heart, and sears the conscience as with a hot iron. It comes, as did the tempter, with gifts in its hands, of rule, of power, and of wealth, to all who will fall down and worship it. They who yield have peace and praise. They who refuse must fight a terrible foe. The cry has been for peace. The lips of some of the ministers and members of the Church of Christ have been padlocked. Politicians, in the grasp of this power, are unable or unwilling to move. They clank their chains with delight, and glory in being allied with an organism so potential and so astute. Others see the peril, and withstand its open and determined advance. No longer now is the clash of arms heard. The city is not, to human sight, a camp of armed men, as in the days of civil war; but if eyes could be opened as were those of the prophet's servant, when horses and chariots were circling in the air, proofs of a conflict might now be discerned, more desperate than was ever fought by flesh and blood on the earth. To-day the "City of Magnificent Distances "resembles the child in the presence of the snake. It is being charmed by the viper. Duty demands that the truth be told which shall break the back of the monster. "Why Priests Should Wed" uncovered the pollutions of Romanism in the hope of saving the women and girls of the Roman Catholic Church, now held in the grasp of superstition. "Washington in the Lap of Rome" appeals to mankind. The surrender to Rome of the Capital of the Great Republic means death to liberty. The people of all lands and climes are interested in the conflict. The facts given will ripen the indignation of pure-minded men and women against the Jesuitical foe, who no longer creeps under cover or hides in the shadow of some wall, but stalks boldly forth on his errand of wickedness. It is believed that it will cause lovers of liberty to shake themselves from their lethargy, and not only take Washington out of the lap of Rome, but throttle the monster threatening the future of the Republic, and lift the nation to its rightful place as the educator of mankind, the leader of the best thought, and the personification of God's great purpose, in placing within the area of an ocean-washed Republic a free Church in a free State.

May God help the truth, is the prayer of

JUSTIN D. FULTON.

1

The Jesuit University In the New Light

ROMANISM IS BEGINNING TO UNCOVER its hand in America. It begins to be fearless, now that it is becoming natural. It is attempting to do here what it has achieved in Europe, to awe the state, control the people, and banish liberty.

Slowly, stealthily, with the look of a saint for the outward seeming, with the heart of a Jesuit for the inward reality, Romanism has accomplished in fact, if not in name, what in name as well as in fact she achieved in so many of the kingdoms of Europe, a union of Church and State. This few will admit, but all may know that fact was to have been revealed on the 24th of May, 1888; that it was not, was not Rome's fault, but God's decree. Preparations had been going on for months to lay on that day, in the presence of the distinguished representatives of the nation, the corner-stone of "the Catholic University of America, that the light of virtue and science might be preserved in the State," in accordance with (he decrees and behests of Rome. The Cardinal, the Prince of the Roman Catholic church who was to officiate as President of the Board of Trustees, is, by virtue of his high office, the most conspicuous figure in the Catholic church in this country. Born of Irish parents, July 23rd, 1834, in Baltimore, and accompanying his father to Ireland as a child, where he received his early education, he returned to the United States and graduated from St. Charles College, Howard Co., Md., in 1857. He then studied theology in St. Mary's Seminary, Baltimore, and was ordained a priest June 30th, 1861. Seven years later he was consecrated bishop of North Carolina. Afterwards he took up his abode in Richmond, Va., and in 1877 became co-adjutor of Archbishop Bayley, of Baltimore, and upon his death became his successor. After the death of Cardinal McCloskey he was appointed to his present exalted position, and carried to it great versatility of talent, an unconquerable energy, and much learning

Gen. W. S. Rosecrans, Grand Marshal, was born in Ohio in 1819, graduated from West Point in 1842, and in the Civil War rose from the position of colonel to corps commander. In 1867 he resigned from the army, went to California, was elected to Congress, and at the expiration of his term was appointed Register of the Treasury. His brother was a bishop of the Roman Catholic church, and he has been noted for his devotion to his church, whether as soldier, congressman, or citizen. The orator of the day, Rev. J. L. Spalding, was born in Lebanon, Ky., in 1840. Educated in Emmetsburg, Ind., St. Mary's, Cincinnati, and in Louvain, Belgium, on May 1st, 1877, he was consecrated bishop of Peoria. He is a scholarly man, and it has been his dream for years to have a great Catholic University built in the United States. It was through him that Miss Mary Gwendolen Caldwell made known her gift of $300,000 to the prelates of the Baltimore Council. The mother of Miss Caldwell was a member of the Breckenridge family. The father amassed a large fortune in New Orleans, and in 1863 was compelled to come North. Residing in New York, the daughter was educated at the Academy of the Sacred Heart, Manhattanville, New York, after which she travelled extensively in Europe. The father, at his death, left an estate of four million dollars, to be divided between his two daughters. The Rev. John J. Keane, the Rector of the University, was born in Ballyshannon, Co. Donegal, Ireland, Sept. 12th, 1839. He studied classics at St. Charles College, Baltimore, and subsequently pursued a full course in St. Mary's Seminary, and was ordained in 1866. For many years he served as assistant of St. Patrick's church, Washington, and in 1878 he was appointed to the See of Richmond. Bishop Keane's zeal, scholarship, eloquence and organizing ability led to his election as a rector of the University. He has raised $800,000 to endow it.

In 1882 Bishop Spalding visited Rome, and obtained the Papal approval. The proposition was discussed by the Archbishops, called to Rome in 1883, and in 1884 the sanction and benediction of the Pope was promulgated to the Plenary Council in Baltimore. It was expected that the Cardinal, dressed in the red robes of his office, arm-in-arm with the President of the United States, was to strike the blow which would inaugurate the commencement of an enterprise that would exert a felt influence upon the institutions of this fast-growing Republic. Soldiers, belonging to an army seven hundred thousand strong, now enlisted and drilled, and being led by the scarred veterans of the Confederate and Union armies, were to be there, under the command of Mayor General Rosecrans, Grand Marshal, who, with prancing steed and nodding plume, was to place before the eyes of gathered thousands the proof that Church and State were united, and that a willing soldiery were getting ready to enforce the decrees of Rome. Bands of music accompanied the delegations, and filled the air with martial strains, as on Wednesday evening they marched along the streets of Washington.

Archbishops, bishops and priests, monks and nuns and Christian brothers, crowded the homes of expectant Romanists. Everything was apparently for Rome. The President of the United States left the Presbyterian Assembly in Philadelphia to grace with his presence this occasion. Every member of the cabinet and distinguished statesmen were expected to keep him company. Seats were prepared on the platform for two thousand guests.

That night, in a great hall in Washington, gathered a company of praying people. They saw the peril; they declared it, and pleaded with God to bring confusion upon the enemies of the faith; though ministers in Washington as a rule, and the churches almost without exception, recognize the Roman Catholic church as a part of the Christian world, and are opposed to saying anything, or having anything said, that shall provoke discussion, or awaken enmity. Many there are who believe that Romanism is the foe of Christianity, and is yet to be cast down.

Thursday morning came. The day darkened as it climbed towards noon; the rain came first as a protest. It increased in quantity, and finally fell in sheets. The streets looked like rivers. The procession was abandoned; the town was held in the grip of the storm. The crowd that gathered about the great stand was roofed with umbrellas. The cardinal and clergy, who expected to pass around the building to bless the foundations, were unwilling to face the storm. At three P.M., a

CHANGE OF PROGRAMME

was announced, in these words: "3 P.M. The procession has been abandoned; but the rest of the ceremony will go on." It did not go on! The foundations remained unblest! As Burns said:

> "Full mony a plan of mice and men
> Gang oft a-glee."

It is not the first time that Jehovah, by storm and rain, has disconcerted and broken up the plans of Rome. Twice this was done in the days of Napoleon; when, but for them, he would have been master of the world. But it came and piled his ships on the lee shore, and buried sailor and soldier in a watery grave.

Once this same terrible result was reached when Philip II. of Spain sent his Armada of ships to crush out the power of Elizabeth, England's noble queen. In our own land, a storm helped us, when hope had almost died out of the heart. In the Old South church, Boston, there stood up the man of God to pray. Liberty was imperilled. A fleet was on its way from the Old World to the New, bearing soldiers, determined to make an end of the attempt to kindle on the shores of this Western World the light of a new-born hope. The wind, that gently lifted a lock of his white hair from his brow, was but the touch of that tempest that engulphed the fleet in ruin and saved the country from peril. That Being who permitted the persecution of the children of Israel until Pharaoh was beside himself with wrath and egotism, and, as if to defy God, followed the people in their march to Canaan, until the floods environed him, when God withdrew the unseen walls which held back the sea and permitted the waters to break forth, smiting horse, men, and riders with the wrath of God, until chariot-wheel crushed into chariot-wheel, and Pharaoh's host, with all their pride and pomp, sank into the bottom of the sea "as a stone," still lives, and Rome, that in spite of warnings and remonstrances had attempted to dominate our intellectual forces, was compelled to halt, and learned again that the "Lady of the Tiber" was to suffer mortification and chagrin, as her beautiful garments were dispoiled by the rain—the good rain, that made the meadows glorious, and opened flowers for the coming sun, and that did for Romanism in the United States what the storm did for the Armada in the Channel. The Cardinal that could make the son of a Presbyterian minister bow to Rome — that could touch a spring and send seven millions of people in America to obey the behests of Leo XIII., could not control God. "Sing unto the Lord a new song, for he hath triumphed gloriously; "and, in answer to prayer, thwarted the scheme to make an impression by a pageant we do not need, and will not always brook.

It was understood that the corner-stone of the building would be laid, no matter what sort of weather prevailed, so members of the Catholic societies and others went bravely on in the rain, attending to the duties assigned them. The bishops assembled at Father Chapelle's residence at two o'clock, where they took carriages with the cardinal and his attendants, and they were driven to the Middleton estate, next to the Soldiers' Home, which they had purchased for $27,000. It has a picturesque and commanding location. An old-fashioned driveway, between rows of trees, leading to the old house, starts from the intersection of Lincoln avenue with the Bunker Hill road. The grounds extend to the Metropolitan Branch of the Baltimore and Ohio Railroad, and the railroad station of Brooks is located there. The distance from the city is two and a-half miles. So out they went, hoping against hope, that the rain would cease.

The ecclesiastical ceremony at the site of the University was planned as follows: The procession was to form at three o'clock along the Bunker Hill road. The various divisions were to gather in fields on both sides of the railroad, in such manner that the first division, when it files out, will pass before all the divisions, and each division in turn will march out upon the road, so that the whole long procession will pass in review before the last division, composed of the bishops and clergy. Following an ecclesiastical custom, each division is arranged with the junior organization first. Thus the youngest parish is placed at the head of the division, composed of representatives of parishes, and the oldest last. In the division composed of the clergy, the different bodies are arranged according to their ecclesiastical rank, the Christian Brothers coming first, followed in order by the priests, the bishops, the archbishops, and last by the Cardinal, the highest dignitary. In the programme it was arranged to sing Haydn's anthem, "The Heavens are Telling," the choir to be accompanied by the full Marine Band. The *heavens told*, without the song, that America has no need of a Papal university, built to perpetuate the dominion of Romanism and to unify the many elements of which the Roman Catholic church in America is composed. One feature of the institution is the establishment of "University Burses." The "Burse" is a fund out of which the poor students are cared for. Every person is at liberty to contribute to it whatever sum he or she may desire. The object is to aid any bright-minded man whose appetite for scholarly attainment in the scientific, or the historical, or the mathematical fields of knowledge are known, but not brought out because of the lack of means to develop them. The reason for locating the university at Washington was ostensibly, as urged by Father Chapelle, because the Capital is growing rapidly as a social, as well as a political centre; that its literary circle is a growing and a liberal one; that a great general library, a superb law library, scientific works and collections, the National Museum, the Observatory, and other public institutions, offered facilities for study that could not be secured elsewhere. In fact, it is the dream of Romanists to make Washington the Rome of America. The Capitol is to be the Vatican; the great Department buildings, the homes of her oligarchy, when the Tiber there, as in the Seven-hilled City of Italy, shall give name to the mistress of the Republic which hopes to be mistress of the world; and when this result is achieved, it would be in keeping to have the Catholic University of America located at that centre of Mary's Land.

It was Thursday evening, May 24th, 1888. A company of lovers of American institutions were gathered in one of the corridors of a great hotel. In came the man who had led the meeting for prayer, and whose face looked as though victory was in the air. He had been all day with the Jesuits. He had seen their discomfiture, and witnessed their mortification, wrath and desperation.

"What is the outlook?"

"All right."

"How goes the fight?"

"Never better. Rome has met her Waterloo, and has received a blow she will not soon forget. Cardinal Gibbons finds that he cannot manage God. He is beaten. The archbishop, bishop, and priests realize it. The president, cabinet, and congressmen who have bent the supple hinges of the knee, that thrift might follow fawning, now see it. Whiskey flows as free to-night as water fell to-day. It is appalling to hear the profanity. Between yesterday and to-day what a change! Then all was hope; now all is gloom! A leading priest, who invited the speaker to come and witness the ceremony, is despondent enough. The minister reminded him of the prophecy, read to him from Revelation 18: 16, and, changing it, said: 'Alas, alas, that great company, clothed in fine linen and purple and scarlet and decked with gold and precious stones and pearls, in one hour have been brought to see their helplessness when contending with the Almighty. May it not be a type of the disasters to attend the enterprise? A bad start is a prophecy of what, at least, is possible. The charter—the organism,—all will be opposed. 'The Lord also shall roar out of Zion, and the heavens and the earth shall shake; but the Lord shall be the hope of his people, and the strength of the children of Israel. So shall ye know that I am the Lord your God, dwelling in Zion, my holy mountain.' All recognized how the mighty angel may cast Rome down as a stone is thrown into the sea when the truth gets before the people, and the machinations of this foe of liberty are understood."

Tongues were loosened. Rome, though mighty, was not almighty. The truculency of politicians had been of no avail. The president and cabinet went home chagrined; better, if not wiser, men.

The Great University looked well on paper; but looked very diminutive to those standing in the mud and rain. So will it be when

15

God shall take Rome in hand. "How much she hath glorified herself and lived deliciously; for she saith in her heart, I sit a queen, and am no widow, and shall see no sorrow. Therefore shall her plagues come in one day, death, mourning, and famine; and she shall be utterly burned with fire: for strong is the Lord God who judgeth her."

Thus spoke the minister to his friend, the priest. The words shook him up. They loosened the foundation on which superstition had been building. The New was coming. The battle was on. Never did a fiercer conflict rage in Washington. The forts were dismantled after the war. Soldiers in blue and gray had gone far away; yet the city was full of combatants. Months before in a Roman Catholic institution, concerning which a war of words seems to go on from year to year, the minister met the priest. They sat at a table with distinguished Romanists, priests and laymen. Eleven nuns waited on them. After dinner, this priest, distinguished for his courage, cultured, talented, eloquent, made a speech, which presents the doings of the church as seen by Romanists. He praised Rome for what she is, and for what she has achieved. He spoke of the proofs of her greatness, seen in her magnificent cathedrals and churches in all the large cities,—the great monasteries, convents, and asylums, crowning the hilltops that look down upon many of our large cities, of the Golden Cross that greets the eye as the traveller passes through the Golden Gate on the California Coast; while in New York, the gateway of the Western World, Rome, in churches, in schools, in convents, in monasteries, in protectories, and what not, leads all other churches in enterprises and in far-reaching plans.

He claimed that there was more money and more brain under the control of the church in New York than in Rome itself, and that now, while the school system was being shattered and the parochial school had become a fact, Rome was to get control of the youth of America, and could hold her own against all comers. He then spoke with pride of the gift of the descendant of the great opponent of Romanism, the gifted Dr. Breckenridge, whose $300,000 was but the seedling—the germ—out of which was to come an University that would surprise and astound the world." He sat down, roundly applauded. The chairman then asked the minister if he would like to speak. Consenting, he arose, and said: "The speech of the distinguished priest gladdens you. Make the most of it, while you have it; it is but for a short time." "What do you mean? Simply this: There is nothing God Almighty hates as he does Romanism. In 1870 you proclaimed your Pope an infallible God. That act proved him to be 'the man of sin, the son of perdition, who opposeth and exalteth himself above all that is called God, or that is worshipped ; so that he as God sitteth in the temple of God, showing himself that he is God.'" Thus was the "wicked revealed, whom the Lord shall consume with the spirit of His mouth, and shall destroy with the brightness of His coming."

"Is that your idea?" shouted the priest.

"That is the word of God. By it men and nations are to be judged. You remember that your Pope had hardly been made the church, when the beast Louis Napoleon, on which he rode into power, was destroyed. Then Babylon fell, because of a power which came down from heaven, and which lightened the earth with its glory. Because of this, the cry is going forth as never before: 'Come out of her, my people, that ye be not partakers of her sins, and that ye receive not of her plagues'! Clouds, dark with the wrath of God, are gathering in the sky of Rome; 'for her sins have reached unto heaven, and God hath remembered her iniquities.'

"Gentlemen, you may not know it, but it is true, that God keeps in his ear the cry and shriek of every Waldensian thrown over the Alpine cliff and torn by the jagged rocks; every body wrenched in twain by the rack of the Inquisition; every woman whose feet were burned over the brasier of coals; every martyr who ascended to heaven in his chariot of fire; all are remembered; and God says: 'Reward her even as she rewarded you, and double unto her double according to her work' in the cup which she hath filled, fill to her double.'

"Then, again, gentlemen, there is a prophecy linked to a fact, to which I have never seen attention called. You have a perfect passion to place all your institutions on elevations. You seek to 'exalt' yourselves in the eye of the people. The Pope 'exalteth himself above all that is called

God, or is worshipped'; and you manifest the same spirit in the location of your public buildings. Our Lord said: 'Whosoever exalteth himself shall be abased.' Every hilltop crowned with your great structures, proclaims the abasement of the Roman Catholic Church, and even now Christ may have said, 'Because you have tried to exalt yourselves at the expense of humanity and of brotherly kindness, *thou shall be brought down to hell.*' 'He that humbleth himself shall be exalted.' This is the outlook for Rome. The present condition is not what you paint it. They tell me, if the mortgages were foreclosed on the property Rome claims to own in New York City, she would not have one foot of land, a convent, or a church. What you own would not pay what you owe. Rome is to be uncovered, and then she will be hated. In the battle to be fought, our hope is in God, and you must look out for great defeats."

With that conversation in mind, there was meaning in the results of the day. The priest felt it. He spoke of his disappointment.

"It is hard to contend against an Almighty must," replied the minister; "the hour approaches when Rome shall be fought by Romanists. What means this unrest of the Pope,—this feeling that he must get out of Italy and find a refuge somewhere else? Does he not know,—does not the world recognize the fact,—that Romanism is nothing without Rome? Let the Pope come to the United States and he would be compelled to walk down Broadway with a stovepipe hat, as Romanists are compelled to wear citizens' clothes in Mexico. The current of free thought in America will take care of Romanism. The time is coming when men will be ashamed of the name in which they pandered to Rome." A minister of distinction declines to attack the Roman Catholic Church in Washington, lest offence be given to the representatives of foreign governments, who crowd St. Matthew's on the Sabbath, and the places of pleasure during the week, for Washington is in the lap of Rome. A Cunarder put out from New England for New York. It was well equipped; but in putting up a stove in the pilot box, a nail was driven too near the compass. You know how that nail would affect the compass. The ship's officer, deceived by that distracted compass, put the ship two hundred miles off her right course, and suddenly the man on the lookout cried: "Land ho!" and the ship was halted within a few yards of her demolition on Nantucket shoals. A sixpenny nail did that; because it was not known that it was misplaced. It shall be the fault of those who will not heed a warning if this Jesuit University shall derange the American compass and send the Ship of State upon the rocks which threaten her.

Shall it be encouraged? It is but a part of a movement to take control of educational interests in the United States. There are 6,800 Roman Catholic churches in the United States, and there are more than 4,000 parochial schools. A movement has begun, to take possession of our public school buildings. Rome withdraws her children from the public school, leaving the seats unoccupied. Then she rents the empty building, and fills it with her children, through the assistance of men elected to do her bidding; as is done in Pittsburg, Pa., and Maiden, Mass. As has been said, Rome sees clearly the peril which confronts her from secular teaching, and from this day she will spare no effort to keep her children within sound of her own bell and within the limits of her own instruction. There will be no compromise; there is no evasion; open, determined and persistent antagonism to our common-school system is henceforth the attitude and policy of the Roman hierarchy. He who hopes to escape this struggle, or out-manoeuvre this foe is already beaten; he does not know the antagonist with whom he is fighting.

The universal diffusion of Catholic education means something more than the opening of schools in every parish; it means a steady and unrelenting attack on our common schools; not on that abstract thing called the common-school system, but on every school in every locality where the Catholic voting population has any strength. This result was inevitable; Catholics have the same indisposition to pay taxes which characterizes the great majority of men of all faiths. They are compelled to support their own church schools; they are not disposed to support the common schools in addition; wherever the way is open they will, as a matter of course, use their power to control or cripple the common schools. The great struggle between our schools and this vigilant and uncompromising foe will not be fought out in Congress or in

Legislatures, in newspapers or pulpits; it will be fought in every school district in the country. There will be no great and decisive battle; there will be a long series of skirmishes.

Every school meeting will be contested, and on the result of these minor contests the struggle itself will turn. Henceforth eternal vigilance will be the price we shall pay for our common schools; henceforth, no man who cares for his community or his country can afford to shirk a duty which has been more honored in the breach than in the observance.

In many communities these foes of the common school will not lack for allies, who will, consciously or unconsciously, work with and for them; men who will fail to see that they are being used as tools by a power which has never yet failed of the highest sagacity in using those who are too shortsighted or too selfish to comprehend the real issues involved. The only reply which must be made to the establishment of the parochial school must be the increased efficiency of the common schools.

The actual Ruler of this nation lives not in the White House at Washington, but in the palace of Baltimore. No important editorial affecting the Romish Church is printed until it has been submitted to the Cardinal for his criticism. We wonder at the power exercised. No member of Congress enters Washington but he is weighed in the Romish balances. If he comes down with the shekels for the church and with votes for her policy, all is well. If not, there is a reckoning-time sure to come, and an influence is exerted at once that touches the springs of power in his far away home. As a political machine, Rome is a transcendent success: and the Jesuit was more than half right when he said, "The representative of the Pope in the Vatican is the Ruler of the United States of America."

2

Romanism A Deception and A Fraud

ROMANISM, AS A RELIGION, IS a deception and a fraud. Jesuitism is the power that propels and controls it. These two facts, made plain to the people, will destroy the reverence felt for Romanism as a part of the religious world, and will take away the sentiment that it has a right to live and act in accordance with its genius and spirit. Then they will be prepared to weigh the proofs which show it to be an enemy, attempting to subvert the foundations of Republican liberty, destroy quietly the public school system, and make the United States of America a Romish Reservation. The claim is, that the Roman Catholic Church is the mother of all churches, that she is the only true church; and, being such, is the Catholic, or Universal Christian Church. That, by Divine appointment, the Apostle Peter was the head and foundation of the church, its Pope and Christ's vicar, or visible representative, on the earth. That he, Peter, lived in Rome for the last twenty-five years of his life, during which time, as the possessor of the "keys" committed to him by the Saviour, he bound or loosed, opened or shut, in heaven, earth, hell, and purgatory, as seemed right in his sight. That each Pope since then is the true successor of St. Peter, invested with equal authority and power; and that to be subject to him and in full and hearty connection with the church he personally, or through the authority he delegates to others, rules, is necessary in the highest degree to salvation. Opposed to this claim, are a few facts:

1. *Rome's pretension to being the mother-church is a deception, because it never was in existence until A. D. 606.* The Acts of the Apostles, as well as all ecclesiastical history, teaches, that the church in Jerusalem, in its origin, in its constitution, takes first rank. John addressed "the seven churches which are in Asia." These churches are—each are—represented by a

golden candlestick, or lamp, separate and distinct one from the other, and not as one lamp; which would have been the case had there existed any just ground for the claim of Home.

2. *For the supremacy of Peter there is no Scriptural warrant.* Peter was in no way the leader of the church. The power and authority conveyed by the appointment of the Apostles was conferred upon all of them. They were all chosen the same way, equally empowered to preach and baptize, all equally entrusted with the power of binding and loosing, all invested with the same mission and equally furnished with the same gifts of the Holy Ghost. Rome contends, not only for a primacy of order, but of power. Fortunately for his own reputation, Peter never did this. When the Mother of Zebedee's children wished it, Christ said, "The Kings of the Gentiles exercise lordship over them, and they that are great exercise authority upon them. But ye shall not be so; but whosoever will be great among you, let him be your servant." Nothing would have so injured Peter with Christ and his brethren, and degraded and disgraced him, as to have done what Rome claims he did do, viz.: claim a pre-eminence among the Apostles.

Peter's name is not always mentioned first. James, Paul, and Apollos' are placed before his, very frequently. Was any one prominent for being dear to Christ? John bore the name of "the beloved disciple." Peter called himself a "fellow-laborer," and expressly forbids the governors of the church to lord it over God's heritage, and bears the rebuke of Paul, because he was to be blamed; without a thought of asserting his superiority or authority. Rome claims that in the words, "Thou art Peter, and upon this rock I will build my church; and the gates of hell shall not prevail against it," our Lord declared Peter's contemplated supremacy. It has sometimes seemed strange that Rome should utterly ignore the other address made to Peter in the same chapter, when Peter assumed supremacy, and Christ said to him: "Get thee behind me, Satan; thou art an offense unto me; for thou savourest not the things that be of God, but those that be of men." Matt. 16: 23. These words apply to Peter, and apply to those who have tried to exalt him above his brethren. The former do not apply to him as being the one upon whom Christ should build his church; for Christ referred to the faith which saw in Him the Son of God. This view was held by Jerome, Chrysostom, Origen, Cyril, Hilary, Augustine, and many more; and Paul, in 1 Cor. 3: 11, points to Christ, in the words: "For other foundation can no man lay than that is laid, which is Christ Jesus." Eph. *2:20:* "And are built upon the foundation of the apostles and prophets, Jesus Christ himself being the chief corner-stone." Then, as to the power of binding or loosing, the position of Rome is confuted by the uniform action of all the apostles on such matters. They declared the conditions of salvation to be repentance towards God and faith in the Lord Jesus Christ, and they would receive the remission of their sins. This precludes the idea that the Romish priesthood have power to absolve from sin.

3. *Romanism is a deception, because it rests its claim upon the false supposition that Peter lived in Rome.* The Scriptures declare that Peter went East, rather than West; lived and wrought in Asia Minor; preached to the churches in ancient Babylon, from which place he wrote his epistle. Romanists want it written at Rome, and insist that Peter went to Rome in A.D. 42; that he was crucified head-downwards in A.D. 67; that he suffered imprisonment in the Marmentine prison, over which towers St. Peter's; that he was buried in the Vatican, where the Pope now lives; while there is not a scintilla of evidence to support the pretension that Peter ever was in Rome. Tradition takes the place of history, and clings to the deception as if it had a basis of even possible fact.

According to the Bible, Peter preached in Jerusalem, and instead of giving orders to the other apostles, as the head of the church, he was sent as a simple missionary to preach with John in Samaria. Acts 8:14. He proclaimed the Gospel in Cesarea, in Antioch, and Babylon, but did not come into the West.

When Paul in A.D. 60 wrote his epistle to the Romans he saluted many, but he did not salute Peter, a sufficient proof that he was not in Rome.

In 61 Paul arrived in Rome and the brethren went out to meet him on the Appian way, Acts 28:15, but Peter was not among them. From the year 61 to 63 Paul wrote from Rome his epistles to the Philippians, Colossians, and to Timothy. In these letters he speaks of many persons, even unknown ones, and no mention is made of Peter.

In his second Epistle, 2 Tim. 4:6, he says: "At my first answer no one stood with me, but all men forsook me." If Peter had been in Rome and free, would he have abandoned Paul? If in prison, would not Paul have referred to him? All this proves that he was not in Rome. The Apostle of the Circumcision never was in Rome. He lived and died in the East. So speaks history. Romanism becomes a fraud when it thus unblushingly lifts a lie into the place of the truth, and demands of those who belong to it unflinching submission and unswerving obedience, from beginning to end.

4. Romanism is a deception, because it predicates salvation, not through the atoning blood of Christ, but upon saying: "I believe that there is here upon earth an organized body that is more than human, because it has a divine commission, and that organized body can teach me the truth, and that in so receiving it I cannot possibly be led into error. I believe that this organism is none other than the Catholic church, directed by the Pope, as the successor of St. Peter, and the moment a man says that, he is a Catholic." The essence of Romanism is summed up in this: *"Subjection of the intellect to divine authority in matters connected with religion."*

Notice, it does not refer to a belief in Jesus Christ, as "the way, the truth, and the life"; nor to receiving him into the heart, that power may be obtained to become a child of God. It makes the church authority the author of life and hope. The millions of Romanists are ruled by a Pope, claimed to be infallible, exalted above all that is called God, and worshipped as was the Druid of our ancestors, or the *Pontifex Maximus* of ancient Rome, and claiming to stand at the top of the system. All the persons in the Godhead, Popery denies. It denies God the Father, by installing the Pope as the Divine vicegerent, by whose authority the Second Commandment, forbidding the worship of images, is trampled upon ; and installs the Pope as Divine vicegerent of the world and the infallible ruler of the conscience. It presents him high and lifted up,

24

clothed with power to annul laws, abrogate treaties, plant and pluck up nations, and do away with the precepts of the moral law. Popery writes on the Papal chair: "This is the seat of God, the throne of the Infallible and Holy One; he who sits here can pardon or retain men's sins, save or destroy souls."

Popery ignores Jesus Christ the Saviour, and worships Mary instead. It robs Christ of his priestly office, by offering the Mass—the priests' sacrifice,—not Christ, to save the sinner. It destroys the prophetical office, by presenting itself as the infallible teacher of the word of God and the only authorized expositor of the true sense of Scripture. It robs Christ of his kingly office, by exalting the Pope to his seat of absolute power and head of the church. In his vesture and on his thigh the Pope has written: "I am King of kings and Lord of lords."

For the Holy Spirit, popery substitutes the sacraments, through which divine blessings are communicated to the soul. It is this impious suggestion which crowds the church with votaries at the various masses, for the deluded believe there is no help for them apart from the priesthood,—the only channel of communication between God and man. It is because of this murderers, no matter how heinous their crime, find it not difficult to espouse Romanism and put the eternal interests of their souls into the keeping of this error. "They believe a lie that they may be damned." Here then is what professes to be a complete church, and yet is an out-and-out counterfeit. Every element of strength and every principle of evil that were found in the ancient idolatries, live over again in the papacy. That same paganism whose cradle was rocked in Chaldea,—whose youth was passed amid the olive groves and matchless temples of Greece,—and whose manhood was reached amid the martial sounds and iron organizations of Rome, has returned anew in this papacy, bringing with it the old rites, the old festivals, the flowers, the incensings, the lustral water, the vestments, the very gods—but with new names ; everything, in short, so that were an old pagan to rise from the dead, he would find himself among his old environments; and, without a moment's doubt, would conclude that Zeus, the ancient Jove, the father of Clio, whose mother is Mercury, answering to Christ and

Mary, was still reigning, and was being worshipped by the same rites that were practised in his honor three thousand years ago.

5. *Romanism is a fraud, because it substitutes a Pantheon of idols for the Christian church, extinguishing the light of revelation, and placing the world back amid the ideas, the deities, and the rites of early idolatrous ages.* It rejects the New Birth and change of heart, and inducts the child into the church in a state of unconsciousness, and holds him there by education, by training, and by fear. The church assumes control of the individual conscience. It claims to hold the keys of heaven and hell. A Romanist is afraid of the truth even of God's word, and millions dare not read or take into their hands the Bible, lest it may sever their hold upon the church, and so whelm the soul in perdition.

The import of such teaching is to place in the hands of conscienceless men the consciences of millions of men. It is the marvel of the age, that at a period when men boast of their aspirations after progress, such numbers should thus fall as dupes into the slough of the most hopeless stagnation, into a total resignation of the freedom of their wills, of the independent action of their souls, into the amplest acceptance of dogmas, creeds and fables which it is a disgrace even to the darkest ages to have been capable of embracing. None of these things which Rome offers has the slightest atom of the simple but sublime religion of Jesus Christ, who sat upon the mountain-side and taught the noblest truths in the simplest language. They are the old tawdry paraphernalia of worn-out Paganism, refurbished and reintroduced by the most impudent priestcraft that ever palmed itself upon the world.

This it is that men are calling a part of the Religious World. Romanism is Antichrist, pure and simple. Daniel, Paul, and John have described it with the pen of inspiration, and painted it with living colors, and the pictures they made of it hang on the walls of the future, so that every eye can trace its origin, its terrible and damning work, and *its awful doom*. Daniel tells of "the little horn," before which three of the ten horns fell; which signify the ten states under control of imperial Rome. These three horns represented the Exarchate of Ravenna, given the

Pope Stephen I. by Pepin, King of France, in A.D. 755. The second was the Kingdom of the Lombards, subdued by Charlemagne of France, and made over to the Pope in A.D. 774. And the third was the State of Rome itself, which was given the Pope by Louis the Pious.

It was upon the acquisition of these states that the Pope became a temporal ruler. It is said, the little horn "had eyes like the eyes of a man,"—"and a mouth speaking great things,"—"great things against the Most High." Assuming Divine titles, such as "His Holiness"; "Head of the Church"; "Christ's Vicar upon Earth"; "Infallibility," etc., etc. But more than this—assuming to dispose of rewards in heaven and hell, as well as on the earth; changing laws of principles and conduct, and conditions of education; a power to depose rulers, give away states or kingdoms, release subjects from their oaths of allegiance; each of which acts, and all together, being an invasion of God's prerogatives, as the king, ruler, saviour, judge of all men, and, therefore, such was speaking "things against the Most High." His "look was more stout than his fellows,"—causing him to claim supreme control over the church, the state, and the world; compelling his people—cardinals, bishops, priests, or whomsoever they were,—to kiss his feet; and princes, at one time, to hold his stirrup while he mounted his horse; and, in some instances, to lay themselves down that he might put his foot upon their necks. Asserting as Pope Paul and Pius did to Henry of France and Elizabeth of England, that as Pope they had a sovereignty above kings and people, and that, by divine appointment, was over nations and over kingdoms, to root out and to cut down, and to destroy and to throw down, to build and to plant. Further, it is added: "He made war with the saints."

So Paul, in 2 Thess. 2, follows up Daniel and John in Revelation 13; uncovers the beast like unto a leopard, and his feet as the feet of a bear, and his mouth as the mouth of a lion, and the dragon gave him his power and his seat and great authority. Then go on to Rev. 17, and the battle with Rome is described: *"The Lamb shall overcome them; for he is Lord of lords and King of kings; and they that are with him are called, and chosen, and faithful."* This is Romanism that is now being destroyed. The Pope has no longer temporal power. Let God's children all over the world tell the truth, and her and his so-called spiritual power shall be destroyed,—consumed by the spirit of the mouth of our Lord, and by the brightness of his coming, as Christ shall shine in the effulgence of proclaimed truth. Is not this papalism, when it would figure as the religion of Jesus Christ, *& fraud?* If so, say so; and the work of redemption will be accomplished. Let the cry arise: "Come out of her, my people, that ye be not partakers of her sins, and that ye receive not of her plagues."

For those who come out of Rome, there is freedom in Jesus Christ; for those who remain in, there are perils such as have not yet been visited upon any race or class: "For her sins have reached unto heaven, and God hath remembered her iniquities."

3

Jesuitism that Runs the Church of Rome

TO WRITE THE HISTORY OF Jesuitism is to give in detail the record of sanctified scoundrelism, as with the face of a saint and the heart of a devil it has lived and wrought in this world, to do its worst against Christianity, brotherly love, manhood and Tightness.

This is an awful charge. But it is also an awful failure of language when the attempt is made to tell the truth concerning this monster of iniquity. Jesuitism proves that, in human debasement, incarnate fiendishness and devilish capacity for being bad, man in the nineteenth century is equal to any horrid character that may have figured on the historic page.

THE ORIGIN OF THE JESUITS.

A cannon-shot hit the leg of a scoundrel instead of his head, as in Spain he stood before Pampileuno's walls. For religion, catholicity and man, that was the unluckiest cannon-shot recorded in history; for when the tibia of the wounded patient knitted they marvelously supported the body of a man who with the heart of a devil has been permitted to masquerade in the robes of a saint. Those familiar with jail philosophy can well appreciate the impulse which drives the criminal, convicted of thieving or burglary, or murder, and on the verge of the tomb, to indulge in fancies of huger thieving, or a crueler and more infamous murder, and to long for life or unshackled arms that he might become pre-eminently notorious by its enactment. Now such a thought came over the brain of Ignatius Loyola, the founder of the Order, profanely called, of Jesus, and he recovered and was successful. The Jesuit University is built in Washington as Conspiracy Hall, in hopes that liberty may be throttled in its stronghold. Loyola took the name of Jesuits for his Order, because of pretended visions of God, the Father, who is claimed to have appeared visibly to him, and desired His Son, Jesus Christ, who stood by laden with a heavy cross, to take special care of him and his companions, which Christ promised to do. They are dangerous, because they declare no villainy, no treachery, nor cruelty to be criminal, provided it tends to the benefit of their Society.

In 1762, the King and Parliament of France were moved against the Order, and to be satisfied as to the grounds of complaint against it, they appointed a commission, consisting of five princes of the blood, four peers of France, seven presidents of the court, thirteen counsellors of the grand chamber, and fourteen other functionaries. This commission examined one hundred and forty-seven Jesuit authors of celebrity, and in their report they say: "This perversity of the doctrine maintained constantly, and without interruption, by the priests, scholars, and others styling themselves of the Society of Jesus, would destroy the natural law,—that rule of life which God himself has written in the heart of man ; and, as a natural result, would break all the bonds of civil society, *authorize theft, perjury, impurity, the most criminal,* and, generally, every passion and every crime, by teaching secret compensation, equivocation, mental reservation; would uproot every feeling of humanity among men, by favoring homicide and parricide; in fact, would overturn the principles and practices of religion, and substitute in its stead all kinds of superstition, by favoring magic, blasphemy, irreligion, and idolatry.* Clement XIV., in his bull suppressing the Order, declares that it has been censured by Popes Urban XII., Clement X., XI., XII., Alexander VII., VIII., Innocent IX., XII., XIII., and Benedict XII., and then proceeds by saying:

"After a mature deliberation, we do, of our certain knowledge and the fulness of our apostolic power, suppress and abolish the said Society. We deprive it of all activity whatever—of its houses, schools, colleges, hospitals, lands, and, in short, of every place whatsoever, in

---

* Letters of Marcus, pp. 106.

whatever kingdom or province they may be situated. We abrogate and annul its statutes, rules, customs, decrees, and constitutions, even though confirmed by oath, and approved by the Holy See, or otherwise. We declare all and all kind of authority, the general, the provincial, the visitors, and other superiors of said Society, to be forever annulled and extinguished, of whatever nature soever the authority may be; as well in things spiritual and temporal."

Be it remembered, that up to A.D. 1860, this Order of persons had been expelled no less than seventy times from countries in which they had been living and applying their principles, and that these were almost all Roman Catholic countries; and yet they have a most popular church in Washington, a college in Georgetown, and now are building the University, with the countenance of the representatives of the Great Republic, in less than a quarter of a century after their assassination of Abraham Lincoln!

Let us learn how they train men for infamous deeds.

Behold them consecrating the dagger of the assassin for, perhaps, some man now under the ban. The following is the Jesuit's manner of consecrating both the persons and weapons employed for the murdering of kings and princes by them accounted heretics.

The person whose silly reasons the Jesuits have overcome with their more potent arguments is immediately conducted into their *sanctum sanctorum,* designed for prayer and meditation. There the dagger is produced, carefully wrapt up in a linen safeguard, enclosed in an iron sheath, engraven with several enigmatical characters, and accompanied with an *Agnus Dei;* certainly, a most monstrous confutation so unadvisedly to intertwine the height of murderous villainy and the most sacred emblem of meekness together. The dagger, unsheathed, is hypocritically bedewed with holy water, and the handle, adorned with a certain number of coral beads, put into his hand, thereby assuring the credulous fool that as many effectual stabs as he gives the assassinated prince, so many souls he should redeem out of purgatory on his own account. Then they deliver the dagger into the homicide's hands, with a solemn recommendation, in these words:

31

"Elected son of God, receive the sword of Jephthah; the sword of Samson, *which was the jawbone of an ass;* the sword of David, wherewith he smote off the head of Goliath; the sword of Gideon; the sword of Judith; the sword of the Maccabees; the sword of Pope Julius II., wherewith he cut off the lives of several princes, his enemies, filling whole cities with slaughter and blood. Go forth prudently, courageously, and the Lord strengthen thine arm."

Which being pronounced, they all fall upon their knees, and the Superior of the Jesuits pronounces the following exorcism:

"Attend, O ye Cherubim; descend and be present, O Seraphim. You thrones, you powers, you holy angels, come down and fill this blessed vessel—the parricide—with eternal glory; and daily offer to him (for it is but a small reward) the crown of the blessed Virgin Mary, and of all the holy patriarchs and martyrs. He is no more concerned among us; he is now of your celestial fraternity. And thou, O God, most terrible and inaccessible, who yet has revealed to this instrument of thine, in thy dedicated place of our prayer and meditation, that such a prince is to be cut off as a tyrant and a heretic, and his dominions to be translated to another line, confirm and strengthen, we beseech thee, this instrument of thine, whom we have consecrated and dedicated to that sacred office, that he may be able to accomplish thy will. Grant him the habergeon of thy divine omnipotency, that he may be enabled to escape the hands of his pursuers. Give him wings, that he may avoid the designs of all that lie in wait for his destruction. Infuse into his soul the beams of thy consolation, to uphold and sustain the weak palace of his body; that, contemning all fears, he may be able to show a cheerful and lively countenance in the midst of present torments or prolonged imprisonments; and that he may sing and rejoice with a more than ordinary exultation, whatever death he undergoes."

This exorcism being finished, the parricide is brought to the altar, over which, at that time, hangs a picture containing the story of James Clement, a Dominican friar, with the figures of several angels protecting him and conducting him to heaven. This Clement was accounted a blessed martyr for his barbarous murder of Henry III., King of France.

This picture the Jesuits show their cully ; and, at the same time, presenting him with a celestial coronet, rehearse these words: "Lord, look down and behold this arm of thine, the executioner of thy justice; let all thy saints arise, and give place to him;" which ceremonies being ended, there are five Jesuits deputed to converse with him, and keep the parricide company; who, in their common discourse, make it their business, upon all occasions, to fill his ears with their divine wheedles; making him believe that a certain celestial splendor shines in his countenance, by the beams whereof they are so overawed as to throw themselves down before him and kiss his feet; that he appears no more a mortal, but is transfigured into a Deity; and, lastly, in a deep dissimulation, they bewail themselves, and feign a kind of envy at the happiness and eternal glory which he is so suddenly to enjoy; exclaiming thus before the credulous wretch: "Would to God the Lord had chosen me in thy stead, and had so ordained it by these means, that being free from the pains of purgatory, I might go directly, without let, to paradise." But if the persons whom they imagined proper to attempt the parricide prove anything squeamish or reluctant to their exhortations, then, by nocturnal scarecrows and affrighting apparitions, or by the suborned appearances of the Holy Virgin, or some other of the saints, even of Ignatius Loyola himself, or some of his most celebrated associates, they terrify the soon retrieved misbeliever into a compliance with a ready prepared oath, which they force him to take, and thereby they animate and encourage his staggering resolution. Thus these villainous and impious *doctors* in the arts *of murder and parricide,* sometimes by the terrors of punishment, sometimes by the allurements of merit, inflame the courage of the unwary, and, having entangled them in the grooves of sacrilegious and bloody attempts, precipitate both soul and body into eternal damnation.

This is the method by which Jesuits clear themselves from their enemies. How happy, then, must that nation be, where Loyalists flourish!

Add to this the Jesuit's oath, and the peril seems increased: "I do renounce and disown any allegiance as due to any heretical king, prince or state named Protestant, or obedience to any of their inferior magistrates or officers.

"I do further declare that the doctrine of the Church of England, the Calvinists, Huguenots, and of others of the name of Protestants, to be damnable; and they themselves are damned and to be damned that will not forsake the same.

"I do further declare, that I will help, assist, and advise all or any of His Holiness' agents, in any place wherever I shall be, to extirpate the heretical Protestant doctrine; and to destroy all their pretended powers, regal or otherwise.

"I do further promise and declare, that notwithstanding I am dispensed with to assume any religion heretical, for the purpose of propagating of the Mother Church's interest, to keep secret and private all her agents' councils, from time to time as they intrust me, and not to divulge, directly or indirectly, by words, writing, or circumstance whatsoever, but to execute all that shall be proposed, given in charge or discovered unto me, by you, my ghostly adviser, or any of this sacred convent. All this I swear, by the blessed Trinity and blessed Sacrament, which I am about to receive, to perform, and on my part to keep inviolably; and do call all the heavenly and glorious host of heaven to witness these my real intentions, to keep this my oath.

"In testimony whereof, I take this most holy and blessed Sacrament of the Eucharist, and witness the same further with my hand and seal, in the holy convent, this day of A.D.," etc.

This oath evidences that every Jesuit is a traitor to the play, ready at any moment to perform any act that will further the interests of his order. It permits him to be a hypocrite, and to profess religion simply to plot against it and overthrow it. Jesuitism makes religion a pretense and a sham and plotting and rascality a business, and yet it runs the Church of Rome, and is treated by one of the great political parties as an ally worthy of confidence and support. Why were the Jesuits reinstated by Pio Nono, and confirmed in their position by Leo XIII? To answer this question, we must go back to 1868. Then, to take away the States of the Church from the rule of the Pope, was to bring universal crash to every

European empire. Fortunately, Emperor William had no faith in such prognostications. Within the Church of Rome was a conflict as to the propriety of pronouncing the Pope infallible. Discussion went on throughout the Roman Catholic world. The prophecy of Paul, in 2 Thess. 2:3,4, was to be fulfilled; "the man of sin, the son of perdition," was to "exalt himself above all that is called God or that is worshipped; so that he as God sitteth in the temple of God, showing himself that he is God." This was fulfilled in A. D. 1870. Two hundred thousand people have borne Pio Nono to his throne in St. Peter's and worshipped him as God. He is absolute in power. French bayonets uphold his temporal power. It looks as if the Pope was supreme.

Open again the Word of God to Rev. 17:11, and read the doom of Louis Napoleon, "the beast that was," is Napoleon I; "and is not," for there was a time when the Napoleonic power was out of sight and out of mind. After which, Louis Napoleon climbed to power, betrayed Mazzini, and Garibaldi in Italy, became the beast upon which the Harlot of the Tiber rode; "and is the eighth and is of the seven," for it will be remembered, he built on the Napoleonic dynasty, and went to perdition. This is prophecy. Read a page from history. The Minister of France walks in the palace-yard of Emperor William and makes a remark which gives offence. Napoleon had boasted of his prowess, and thought a war only was necessary to make him Master of Prussia, as was his uncle before him. Emperor William resented the affront and rebuked the speaker. As a result, war was declared; and the German army, as if on a picnic excursion, overran France, encamped at Versailles, and took possession of Paris, and Louis Napoleon as an exile disappeared from the affairs of Europe. The army of France was withdrawn. The army of Victor Emmanuel was invited by the people of the States of the Church to enter Rome as King of Italy. He came. The Pope retired to the Vatican as the spiritual sovereign of Roman Catholics, but as temporal ruler no more.

It was to the Pope a humiliation, and, perhaps, prepares the way for his destruction. Without an army, without support, he turned to the only power in the world in which he could trust to do the work of conspirators, assassins, and revolutionists, the Jesuits. He reinstated them. They became the right arm of his strength, and have been seeking his restoration to temporal power. Everyone who knows what their principles and history are, will feel satisfied that, like the Indian boomerang, they are much more likely to injure the hand that uses them than those whom they are employed to oppose. The condition of the Pope is pitiable. He lives, as it were, on sufferance; no longer the mighty and powerful ruler of the past, but influential simply because of his power outside of Rome, not inside. The Bible has entered Rome, the Word of God is not bound.

We have been accustomed to bless God for that fatherly care of Divine Providence, which neither allowed the era of American colonization to be hastened, nor that of the Reformation to be deferred. Had these events been differently arranged, it has been said—had Spanish blood, and not English, flowed in the veins of our first settlers, or had the Mayflower borne to our shores the foundations of a Catholic colony, and had Roger Williams been a Jesuit missionary—or had the schemes of French conquest, that would have made Canada but the starting point of North American empire, been successful, how different had been the annals of the country, and the entire race! All that reads well. But when we remember that Providence, R. I., is almost a Roman Catholic town—that a bishop was recently installed there in the presence of all the magnates of the state, and that Washington is in the lap of Rome, it becomes us not to boast of deliverance, but to recall our peril and prepare to resist the encroachments of liberty's foe. Remember, that the Jesuits ruling Washington may dispense with all laws, human and divine, dissolve all oaths and vows, and free men in the Cabinet of the President from the obligations which bind other men. So soon as a city or country is under their control, no member of the community can promise to himself security, either to his life, honor, or estate. Nay, the person of the President is not exempted from danger, when he is once the object of Jesuitical spleen.

Shall Jesuits be welcomed or expelled? is the question which is yet to agitate the people of the United States. Up to the present time, so great has been the love of liberty in the hearts of the people, that they have tolerated with impunity anarchists, revolutionists, and Jesuits. The idea of suppression for opinion's sake has been repugnant to the sentiment of the majority. But a reaction is setting in. The people begin to see that it is cowardice to throw up the hands at the *dicta* of this blood-stained crowd, and permit them to scuttle the ship on which we are making a common voyage. Self-preservation, if nothing else, will compel the people of the United States to take the most stringent measures against the evil of the time, and to give even clearer scrutiny to the methods and principles and conduct of the Jesuits. They work in darkness, and they oppose the truth. Seven millions of people in free America, and 250,000,000 throughout the world, are ruled by their mandate. The Pope has enthroned them in power and reinstated them in all their former possessions. With the people over whom they have control, argument goes for nothing. The needs of the country are cast aside as unworthy of regard. The requirements of the church is their all and in all. Oaths are valueless, if to keep them imperils the Order, or the church. Their history is a continued series of associations, massacres of innocent people, conspiracies and machinations against existing laws and orders. The masses they have incited to revolt, and the rulers to bloody and fruitless wars. Corruption they sow broadcast over the land in order to further their doctrines of treason, perjury, falsehood, and murder. Brazen as they are, they use their power of religion as a cloak to hide their sins against God, and their sins against man. To-day their one object of detestation is the public school system of the United States. They see that the education of the masses is their ruination. In the South there are millions of freedmen growing up in ignorance, owing to the inability of the several States to educate them. Well has the Hon. Henry W. Blair, in the Senate, called attention to the duty of the nation to educate the rising generation. "It is of very little consequence," said the Senator, "relatively, what becomes of the present generation. What we are, we are, and are likely to be; but it is of great importance what shall be the fate of the future, which depends so largely upon the conduct of the present. The real question is, whether this generation, with natural

37

powers for the control of the destiny of the country for the time being, is to make that provision for the generation to come which has been made for the generation existing by those who have preceded it; whether this generation, so far as it has the capacity to do so, is to make better preparation for the discharge of its duties on the part of the coming generation, so far as it should be made, than was made by those who preceded us." If the Christian and intelligent people of the United States are not awake to the importance of this measure, the Jesuits are. They saw from the first that Romanism is doomed, if the people of this land are to be educated. Jesuitism understands that a great fight is already outlining itself for the future between the common schools of the United States and Romanism. Jesuitism is not afraid. She fights education openly and secretly. Said Senator Blair: "Upon this very floor, soon after we had passed this bill, full two years *ago,* and while it was in the hands of a packed committee in the House of Representatives, where it was finally strangled,—on this very floor, a senator showed me a letter which I read with my own eyes, the original letter of a Jesuit priest, in which he begged a member of Congress to oppose this bill and to kill it, saying, *that* they *had organized all over the country* for its destruction; that they succeeded in the committees of the House, and they would destroy the bill inevitably; and if they had only known it early enough, they could have prevented its passing through the Senate. They have begun in season this time; but they will not destroy this bill.

"Twelve years ago, when I was a member of the House of Representatives, and when we were undertaking to enact a constitutional amendment which was to prevent the appropriation of public money to the support of sectarian schools in this country, a friend of mine pointed out to me upon that floor nine Jesuits, who were there log-rolling against that proposed amendment of the Constitution. There in Washington is that Jesuit organization which has set out to control this country, which has been repudiated by every free country, Catholic and Protestant, in the Old World: they have come to our borders; they are among us today, and to stay; and they understand that they are to secure the control of this continent, by destroying the public school system of

America. They are engaged in that nefarious, wicked work. And as Jesuits have been expelled from the Old World, let me say, the time is soon coming when the Jesuits will be looked upon as more the enemy of this country than is the Anarchist to-day. And the process either of their expulsion, or of their conversion, will be the one in which the American people will sometime be engaged, unless the Order change their programme and their work."

Brave words were these of Senator Blair, the bravest spoken for many a day! The Senate passed the Bill. When it went to the House, the Jesuits again showed their hand. The Presidential election being near, made men careful. The usual Jesuit lobby was present, and the bill was referred to a committee appointed by the Jesuits' servant, the Speaker of the House, where it will lie until the citizens awake to their peril, and send men to Congress less susceptible to Jesuitical influence. The speech was delivered Feb. 15th, 1888. On May 25th, 1888, Mr. Blair introduced the following joint resolution ; which was read twice, and ordered to lie on the table:

JOINT RESOLUTION.

PROPOSING AN AMENDMENT TO THE CONSTITUTION or THE UNITED STATES, RESPECTING ESTABLISHMENTS OF RELIGION AND FREE PUBLIC SCHOOLS.

"*Resolved by the Senate and House of Representatives of the United States of America in Congress assembled (two-thirds of each House concurring therein),* That, the following amendment to the Constitution of the United States be, and hereby is, proposed to the States, to become valid when ratified by the legislatures of three-fourths of the States, as provided in the Constitution:

ARTICLE

"SECTION 1.—No State shall ever make or maintain any law respecting an establishment of religion, or prohibiting the free exercise thereof.

"SEC. 2.—Each State in this Union shall establish and maintain a system of free public schools, adequate for the education of all the children living therein, between the ages of six and sixteen years, inclusive, in the common branches of knowledge, and in virtue, morality, and the principles of the Christian religion. But no money raised by taxation imposed by law, or any money or other property or credit belonging to any municipal organization, or to any State, or to the United States, shall ever be appropriated, applied, or given to the use or purposes of any school, institution, corporation, or person, whereby instruction or training shall be given in the doctrines, tenets, beliefs, ceremonials, or observances peculiar to any sect, denomination, organization, or society, being, or claiming to be, religious in its character, nor shall such peculiar doctrines, tenets, beliefs, ceremonials, or observances, be taught or inculcated, in the free public schools.

"SEC. 3.—To the end that each State, the United States, and all the people thereof, may have and preserve governments republican in form and in substance, the United States shall guaranty to every State, and to the people of every State and of the United States, the support and maintenance of such a system of free public schools as is herein provided.

"SEC. 4.—That Congress shall enforce this article by legislation when necessary."

Another plot.—The Jesuits have formed a colonization scheme, with a capital of $2,000,000, to aid Romanists in getting control of the South.

THE CONTENTION.

All the Southern States were represented except Florida, Texas and Arkansas, and most, if not all the great Southern railroad corporations were likewise represented by their Presidents or other officers. The following is taken from the Atlanta *Evening Journal* of April 26th, being part of the report of that paper:

40

"Gov. Fitzhugh Lee, of Virginia, was selected as President. Committees on business and resolutions were appointed by the delegations from the respective States. Col. W. P. Price was made the chairman of the Georgia delegation, and Mr. Sandy Cohen, of Augusta, selected as secretary. Governor J. B. Gordon, Bishop Becker, Patrick Walsh, and E. P. Howell, were chosen as the Committee for Georgia. Interesting addresses were made by Cardinal Gibbons, Rt. Rev. Bishop Kane of West Virginia, Rt. Rev. Bishop Northup of South Carolina, and Governors Gordon of Georgia and Richardson of South Carolina. The speech of Gov. Gordon is especially highly commended.

"At the night session, the Immigration Committee adopted the following resolutions:

"*Resolved,* That an Immigration Society be established, with headquarters in the city of New York, to be styled The Southern Immigration Association.

"*Resolved,* That this Association be placed under the care of a board of directors, composed of one member of each Southern railroad or other corporation, trade, industrial or other organization in each state, county, city or town, situated east of the Mississippi river, that will contribute the sum of $1,000 towards the expenses of said Association on or before July 1st next, and that on the second Tuesday of July, 1888, the board so constituted shall meet in New York, and proceed to organize, and adopt such by-laws, rules and regulations as may be necessary for its government.

"*Resolved,* That until such organization is perfected, Major John D. Kelly, Jr., be constituted chief of the Association, with power to call the board together whenever said contributions from railroads or other corporations, trades, industrial or other organizations of states, cities, counties and towns, shall have reached the aggregate sum of $20,000; and when such call has been made, the board of directors shall proceed immediately to perfect a permanent organization, as provided for in the second resolution.

"*Resolved,* That immediately upon adoption of these resolutions, the Secretary of the convention shall give notice of the same to the

Governor of each of the Southern States, to the President of each of the Southern railroads, and to the Mayor of every city, and to every town in the Southern States east of the Mississippi River, having a population of 5,000 or more, and to solicit the co-operation of said officers in furthering the objects of this convention." The central office of this association is located at New York.

Concerning this convention, it is meet that all should be informed. It met April 25, 1888, at Hot Springs, North Carolina. There were present the cardinal, bishops, priests, politicians and railroad men. The object for which the conference was called was the consideration of Catholic immigration to the South.

Slavery, whatever were its evils, fenced off Roman immigration from Europe, and threw it North, so that, of the 16,000,000 foreigners who have come to the country, not more than 600,000 have settled in the Southern States.

It is known that the negroes in the South are Republicans; and if their votes are counted they will become a power. The Jesuits attempt to offset this by a foreign vote. Romanism is advancing through our open gates like a mighty force, bulldozing and corrupting our legislators, and demanding privileges and exemptions for itself which no other sect would do. How long will it be before the Jesuits shall engineer bills through the halls of Congress as they have done in New York?

CARDINAL GIBBONS' VIEWS ON THIS PUBLIC QUESTION.

Cardinal Gibbons has just returned from the South. Regarding the immigration convention held recently at Hot Springs, N. C., he says: "The class of immigrants that the convention wants to bring among the people of the South are thrifty and well-to-do natives of Ireland and Germany. We do not want anarchists or paupers. The South needs development badly, and I know of no better way than to offer inducements to honest emigrants. I deny that the movement is one to increase the power of the Catholic Church in the South, other than what legitimate increase may follow from such. The Church upholds the law, and that should be sufficient guaranty to any intelligent mind of the sincerity and honesty of our purpose." Will the American people be deceived by this Jesuitical special pleading for this Romish scheme?

CAN THE JESUITS BE EXPELLED?

A recent writer has said, that in expelling the Jesuits, not alone all Protestant Americans would unite, but thousands upon thousands of the most intelligent members of the Roman Catholic Church would join hands. *Jesuitism is almost as dangerous to them as to Protestants.* There is no religion in Jesuitism. It is foreign to the principles of the gospel, inimical to liberty, and a conspirator against the State. Because of their insatiate greed for power and influence, they have been feared, hated, driven out. It is believed that it will be so in this, free land. Some deed will be performed, some word spoken, which shall uncover the traitor; when the American people will arise and make short work of the invader that seeks to crush out freedom, that despotism resting on ignorance, on superstition and error, may thrive. The cry will yet be heard: *"Expel the Jesuits."* Then, *vox populi* shall be the *vox Dei.*

4

How Washington Came to be Washington

THIS FEW SEEM TO KNOW; the many reckon, it happened so. Such are oblivious to the fact, that before even Washington was even a dream in the minds of men, Rome had plotted to hold the continent. By Rome, we mean the power that makes Rome what she is, and what she is to be, "the prince of the power of the air," who has incarnated himself in Jesuitism, as Christ is incarnated in Christianity; the power that works in darkness, and plans the suppression of the truth and the overthrow of the rule of Christ. "For we wrestle not," says Paul, "against flesh and blood, but against principalities and powers, and against the rulers of the darkness of this world, against spiritual wickedness in high places."[*] John said: "He that committeth sin is of the devil, for the devil sinneth from the beginning. For this purpose was the Son of God manifested, that he might destroy the works of the devil."[†] In this manifestation of Christ through the proclamation of the truth, lies the hope of the world. If then we charge Romanism with being cunning, subtle, and sly, the reason for the charge is supplied in the words quoted, which inform us of the cunning craftiness whereby Rome lies in wait to deceive.

THE POWER IS UNSEEN.

It is shadowy. It inhabits the air and infects it. Romanism is the malaria of the spiritual world. It stupefies the brain, deadens the heart, and sears the conscience as with a hot iron. It stands across the track of

---

[*] Eph. 6; 12. f 1 John 3 : 8.
[†] 1 John 3:8

44

the world's life, with gifts in its hands, offering rule, supremacy, power and wealth to all who will full down and worship her.*

They who yield have peace and praise. They who refuse must fight a desperate foe. The many do not believe this. They are blinded by ambition and fear, and they see it not. Deaf are they and they hear not the truth, and yet the truth remains. The what is, is the outgrowth of the what has been. Don't forget it. A wise, astute, cunning, comprehensive intellect has helped Romanism in the past, and is helping it now.

Washington is in the lap of Rome, because of influences which stirred the hearts of people and made them to act worse than they knew.

A few facts will make all this plain. Columbus was actuated by a desire to promote the interests of Romanism, when he traversed an unknown sea and discovered this Western World. Cortez and Pizarro went to Mexico and Peru, and captured them for the same purpose. Their lives were full of cruelty, but that did not hurt them with Rome. Lord Baltimore came to Maryland to find a refuge for persecuted Romanists and named the place of retreat Mary's land. To escape the fangs of Romanism and priestly intolerance, the Puritans forsook their homes beyond the sea, came to New England, and on Plymouth Rock built an altar to liberty, sought on bleak New England shores freedom to worship God. They have been called narrow in their thought, and it is claimed they meant by liberty, liberty for themselves, and the right to banish all who thought differently.

Roger Williams, in the furnace fire of affliction and persecution, had the fetters of slavery to creed burned away, and came forth, through the wilderness and the sleet and snows of winter, to "What Cheer Rock," where he became the champion of liberty for all.

Archbishop Hughes once said: "Far be it from me to diminish, by one iota, the merit that is claimed for Rhode Island, Pennsylvania, and perhaps other states, on the score of having proclaimed religious freedom, but the Catholics of Maryland, by priority of time, had borne away the prize." This is untrue, both as regards time and character of

---

* 2 Thess. 2: 8, 9.

what purported to be religious freedom. The Roman Catholic colony sailed up the Potomac in 1634. In Maryland the boasted law was passed in 1649, two years after the doctrine of religious freedom was proclaimed in Rhode Island. Bancroft, in speaking of what was done in Maryland, says: "The controversy between the king and the parliament advanced, the overthrow of the monarchy seemed about to confer unlimited power in England upon the embittered enemies of the Romish Church; and, as if with a foresight of impending danger, and an earnest desire to stay its approach, the Roman Catholics of Maryland, with the covert countenance of their governor and of the proprietary, determined to place upon their statute-book *an act of guaranty of religious freedom,* which had ever been sacred upon their soil. This is the language of the Act: "And whereas the enforcing of the conscience in matters of religion had frequently fallen out to be of dangerous consequences in those commonwealths where it has been practiced, and for the more quiet and peaceable government of this province, and the better to preserve mutual love and amity among the inhabitants, no person within this province professing to believe in Jesus Christ, shall in any ways be troubled, molested, or discountenanced for his or her religion, or the free exercise thereof." This, then, is their law—poor as it is. In Rhode Island, their code of laws passed in 1647, closes with the following noble *avowal of religious liberty to all:* "Otherwise than this what is herein forbidden, all men may walk as their consciences persuade them, every one in the name of God. And let the lambs of the Most High walk in this colony without molestation, in the name of Jehovah their God, for ever and ever."

At a time when Germany was the battle-field for all Europe, in the implacable wars of religion; when even Holland was bleeding with the anger of vengeful factions; when France was still to go through the fearful straggle with bigotry; when England was gasping under the despotism of intolerance; almost half a century before William Penn became an American proprietor; and two years before Descartes founded modern philosophy on the method of free reflection—Roger Williams assisted the great doctrine of intellectual liberty. It became his glory to found a state upon that principle; and to stamp it upon its rising institutions, in characters so deep that the impression has remained to the present day, and can never be erased without the total destruction of the work. The principles which the first sustained, amid the bickerings of a colonial faith, next asserted in the general court of Massachusetts, and then introduced into the wilds of Narragansett Bay, he soon found occasion to publish to the world, and to defend as the basis of the religious freedom of mankind; so that, borrowing the rhetoric employed by his antagonist in derision, we may compare him to the lark, the pleasant bird of the peaceful summer, that, affecting to soar aloft, springs upward from the ground, takes his rise from pole to tree, and at last surmounting the highest hills, utters his clear chorals through the skies of morning. He was the first person in modern Christendom to assert, in its plenitude, the doctrine of the liberty of conscience, the equality of opinions before the law; and in its defense he was the harbinger of Milton, the precursor and the superior of Jeremy Taylor. For Taylor limited his toleration to a few Christian sects; the philanthrophy of Williams compassed the earth. Taylor favored partial reform, commended lenity, argued for forbearance, and entered a special plea in behalf of each tolerable sect: Williams would permit persecutions of no opinion, of no religion; leaving heresy unharmed by law, and orthodoxy unprotected by the terrors of penal statutes.

Without comment, let us notice what Bancroft says of the Maryland statutes:

"The clause for liberty in Maryland," he says, "extended only to Christians, and was introduced by the proviso, 'That whatsoever person shall blaspheme God, or shall deny or reproach the Holy Trinity, or any of the three Persons thereof, shall be punished by death. Any person using any reproachful word or speeches concerning the Blessed Virgin Mary, Mother of our Saviour, or the holy Apostles or Evangelists, or any of them, for the first offense, were to forfeit five pounds sterling to the lord proprietary, or, in default of payment, to be publicly and severely whipped and imprisoned, as before directed; and for the third offense to forfeit lands and goods, and be forever banished out of the province.'"

Cardinal Gibbons defines religious liberty to be "the free right of worshipping God according to the dictates of a right conscience, and of producing a form of religion most in accordance with his duties to God." In other words, religious liberty is the free right of worshipping according to the commands of the church of Rome, and of producing a form of religion in accordance with the commands of the Pope. Behind such a definition the Inquisitorial tortures of Torquemada in Spain were practised, the Waldenses and Albigenses were exterminated by fire and sword, Ridley and Latimer were burned at the stake, the fires were kindled at Smithfield for the burning of the Word of God, and the inhuman barbarities witnessed in convents and elsewhere where Rome has control, are sanctioned and endorsed. Full religious liberty means perfect liberty in our relation to God, to believe or not to believe, to worship or not to worship, as conscience may dictate. In the realm of religious liberty, suasion is the only weapon to be used. God alone is the Lord of the conscience. For this principle Roger Williams, Isaac Backus and others contended, and the doctrines they enunciated have shed a light which causes the thrones of despotism to stand out in horrid contrast with the altars of Republican hope.

After the proclamation of religious liberty came the formation of the Republic. A nation was born. A capital became a necessity. It has been said: " The American capital is the only seat of Government of a first-class power which was a thought and the performance of the Government itself. It used to be called, in the Madisonian era, "the only virgin capital in the world."*

St. Petersburg was the thought of an emperor, but the capital of Russia long remained at Moscow, and Peter the Great said that he designed St. Petersburg to be only a window looking into Europe. Washington City was designed to be not merely a window, but a whole inhabitancy, in fee simple, for the deliberations of Congress, and they were to exercise exclusive legislation over it. So the Constitutional Convention ordained, and in less than seven weeks after the thirteenth State ratified the Constitution, the place of the Capital was designated by

---

* Geo. Alfred Townsend, in his Washington City, Outside and Inside.

Congress to the Potomac River. In six months, the precise territory on the Potomac was selected under the personal eye of Washington. The home of the so-called Father of his Country was Mt. Vernon. Virginia was then the Empire State. Her population outnumbered both New York and Pennsylvania. Baltimore was then the Queen City, and Annapolis offered a safe retreat for Congress, who had been insulted in Philadelphia, and the Pennsylvanian authorities neglected to afford adequate protection. Then Congress resolved to have a place of its own.

Maryland was an early applicant for the seat of Government, and so was Michigan, Kentucky, Indiana; but the Federal City came to Maryland and was located on the banks of the Potomac, very largely because of the munificent offer made by Virginia, and of the paramount influence of Washington. At that time Georgetown was a port of entry, and was a slavemarket, and largely settled by Romanists. The Jesuit College had been established there, and priest and people were quick to see the opportunities of advancement placed within their reach. The influence of Roman Catholic Maryland has been noticeable in the "City of Magnificent Distances" from the first. Behind Maryland, and in league with Jesuit and Priests, was and is the power referred to, "The Prince of the power of the air." This fact must be kept in mind. It explains the mysteries that envelop the city.

Does it not tell us another truth, that God is not afraid. Though Satan is potent, he is not omnipotent. Though Rome is very prudent and wise, she has not all wisdom. Up above us all is a Being who sees the end from the beginning, and though "the lot is cast into the lap, the disposal thereof is with the Lord." Let us believe this. "He that hath a dream, let him tell a dream, and he that hath my word, let him speak my word faithfully. What is the chaff to the wheat? saith the Lord. Is not my word like a fire? saith the Lord, and like a hammer that breaketh the rock in pieces ?"*

It was July 16th, 1790, that President Washington approved the bill in six sections which directed the acceptance of ten miles square for the

---

* Jer. 23:28,29.

permanent seat of the Government. Georgetown had been laid out for forty years. The Jesuit mission of Maryland, began by Father Andrew White, Father John Grovernor and Father Timothy Hayes, in 1633, antedates the settlement of all the original thirteen states, except Virginia and Massachusetts.

The Jesuit College had been founded in 1789, one year before the capital was located on the Potomac. It was chartered as a University in 1815. It had been weak. In 1872, though ten Jesuit professors taught, there were but fifty-six students. The Convent of Visitation was founded in 1799. Virginia was called "the Mother of Presidents, and the Mother of States." She had then a population of 750,000; Pennsylvania had 434,000; and New York 340,000. North Carolina, with 394,000, outnumbered Massachusetts with 379,000. It was not until 1820 that any state passed Virginia; but in 1830 New York and Pennsylvania had bidden her "good bye!"

The Capitol was staked out the year after Franklin died, thirty years before the death of George III., in Goethe's 52nd year and Schiller's 32nd; sixteen years before the first steamboat, two years before Louis XII., was guillotined, when Louis Phillippi was in his 19th year, when George Stephenson was a boy of ten, the year John Wesley died, in Napoleon's 22nd year, the year Morse was born and Mirabeau was buried, in the third year of the *London Times,* just after Lafayette had been the most powerful man in France, three years before the death of Edward Gibbon, while Warren Hastings was on trial, in Burke's 61st year, in Foxe's 42nd, Pitt's 32nd, in the Popedom of Pius VII.

The laying-out of the city was taken in charge by Major L' Enfant. In the survey, the little creek called the Tiber—a name so significant to Romanists; though it designates a little creek, long afterwards the eyesore of the city—obtained significance in the estimation of Roman Catholics.

So much for history. Rumor has it that the Southerners voted against a Northern town, that slavery might find protection beneath the shadow of the Capitol, where she reared her Auction Block, and did her best to perpetuate her infamies. Is it not possible that Rome, the foster-parent of slavery, hoped to find in slaveholders allies and helpers to promote the interests of this twin-relic of mediaeval barbarism, which it is hoped may be removed without a civil war and without compelling the nation to wade through a sea of blood? Victor Hugo, in his *Les Miserables,* describes the devil-fish. Its long, floating arms envelopes its victim, and silently bears it to the vortex of ruin. The devil-fish of Victor Hugo's imagination is matched by the skill displayed by Rome in Washington, which it seeks to hold.

Mighty as is Rome, it has been baffled and beaten elsewhere, and can be beaten again. At this hour, it looks as if an untimely surrender had been made. The truth proclaimed will awaken the people to the infamy of the deed, and they will take back what belongs to them, and Washington shall be free.

5

Jesuits Climb To Power In Washington

JESUITS SUE FOR THE FAVOR of the great and powerful. To obtain this, they decry faith in God, join in attacks on Rome, play the atheist or the infidel. Jesuitism permits its votary to do what pleases him. Submission to God is not in their creed. Jesuitism, in its practice, pays a premium on talent, on trickery, on cunning. It glories in subtlety. It is "all things to all men." Falsehood, theft, murder,—none of these things stand in its way. According to the compendium published in Strasburg in 1843, it is written as follows:

"Perjury—Should it be asked how far a man should be bound, who has taken an oath in a false manner, and for the purpose of deceiving, the answer is, that in point of religion he is not bound at all, because he has not taken a true oath; but in point of justice he is bound to do that which he has sworn fictitiously and in order to deceive." There is honor for the people in America I Robbery is permitted, and so is murder! Jesuitism is free to accomplish its designs. Among the wants of mankind may be reckoned an appetite for deception; a desire inherent in our depraved natures to bring to an agreement the claims of the Deity with the indulgence of our frailties; a mild impatience for the conveniences and splendors of a religious structure in which the history of delusion may be enjoyed to the full. And most prodigally does the Romish church minister to this demand. Ample and complete indeed was the apparatus which she provided for the accommodation of all the various passions and propensities of man.

When the structure which she had reared had reached its perfection, it "had a chamber for every natural faculty of the soul, and an occupation for every energy of the natural spirit." She there permitted every extreme of abstemiousness and indulgence, fast and revelry; melancholy abstraction and burning zeal; subtle acuteness and popular discourse; world renunciation and worldly ambition; embracing the arts and the sciences and the stores of ancient learning; adding antiquity and misrepresentation of all monuments of better times, and covering carefully with a venerable veil that only monument of better times which was able to expose the false ministry of the infinite superstition.*

It is needless to add that the sorcery which thus drugged the world, was, from the first, most prodigally patronized by the vices and wants of human nature. In Washington, nothing is done by Romanists to frighten the most timid. Nothing to waken people up. Nothing to scare or alarm. And yet whoever enters Washington is met by this unseen influence. If he surrenders, be he president, department clerk, or minister of the gospel, there is peace. If he refuses to yield, and stands for the liberties of the people, then there is a fight. The powers of hell are evoked. His path is blocked. His limbs are fettered. His words fall like lead, and are no longer winged with power. This is known; and men who wish promotion recognize the truth, and adjust their plans accordingly.

Rome *as a machine in politics is a success.* The Pope is the church, since 1870. The Jesuits rule the Pope.

It is said that Leo XIII. thought himself to be Pope. The Jesuits thought differently. The Pope was poisoned. His agony was excruciating. A Jesuit approached him; told him the truth: *"You are poisoned. You have so long a time to live. If you surrender, the antidote is ready."* He surrendered to Jesuitism, and lives as their machine, to be worked in their interest, and as the foe of all that is ennobling and improving among men. Does that story seem incredible? It is but a repetition of what has occurred again and again. Jesuitism, that has been banished from every country in Europe, finds in the United States a welcome and a sphere for action. The Cardinal is the mouthpiece and servant of the Order. As a political machine, it is without a rival. It is not hindered by principle or even pretension. It does what it will pay to have done. It works for its own interest, first, last, and all the time. It helps the party

---

* Irving's Babylon, page 238.

that will do its behests blindly and without questioning. It delivers its goods. If it promises votes for reward, it gives the votes and expects the reward. Powerful at Washington, it is equally powerful outside. Offend the Order at the Seat of Government, and a whispered word brings opposition from every quarter, if that be necessary; while it delivers a single blow with equal force, and is feared everywhere, because of its capabilities to work mischief in any given locality.

In the days of slavery, it was the ally of despotism. It was supposed to be the sure ally of the Confederacy; or, perhaps, the attempt to draw out of the Union never had been made. What it could not do openly, it did in secret. The lovers of liberty not only overthrew slavery, but proved to Romanism that the cohorts of liberty are to be feared. Hence Romanism withdrew from public gaze, and, adopting the tactics of Uriah Heep, served that it might rule. The audaciousness of Rome is only equalled by its industry. It never tires. It is in league with all the forces of evil. Three-fourths of the saloonkeepers are Romanists. A politician of Cincinnati declared, "I would rather have the help of one saloon than of five churches." The probability is, the churches could not be brought to the support of such a man. The saloons could. Rome runs them. They pay for it. Week after week, Sisters, in the service of Rome, visit them and obtain their weekly stipend, and bestow the blessing of the church on the infamous traffic.

Rome climbs to power because it is joined to every form of evil, is in league with the enemy of all righteousness, and runs with the multitude in evil-doing. To Rome Satan said, "Fall down and worship me, and I will lift you to places of power and influence." The deed was done. The result has followed. Place, then, an organism that is utterly unscrupulous at the direction of a party, that controls the press and the "plug-uglies," the pulpit and the penal class,—that lays one hand on the homes of fashion and culture, and the other on the tenement-house; one on the banking office, and the other on the workshop and factory,— that marshals the aspirants after power and the class that only cries for gain,—that steps upon the platform as adviser, and into the caucus as director,—that is at all times and everywhere capable of achieving results,—and it is not strange that its power is evoked and that its behests are obeyed. Rome has climbed to power in Washington because men have forgotten country and God, and served evil for the sake of gain. It has been said:

"The Inquisition is not only one of the horrors of history, but one of its greatest lessons also. It is the greatest argument to prove that the only safety of nations is injustice and liberty."

In a few years Rome will become able to establish the Inquisition here, unless a speedy change for the better comes over the spirit of our people. When I looked upon the cells of solid masonry standing back to back in the cellar of a Catholic church in New Jersey, and noticed the size of them, and that they were exactly such ones as are described in history, in which human beings were walled up alive, I said to myself, "Who is to be walled up to die in there?" I stood upon the wall of an unfinished church, to take my observation—that wall was several feet thick. A woman was wheeling a baby-carriage upon it, and she had plenty of room. Not the cry of a hundred men could be heard through such a wall when finished. What do innocent churches want of such walls in a free country? Ah! the not distant future will tell, if "the Catholics become a considerable majority."

That kind of a cell is not confined to New Jersey. The cells and underground passages in the cellar of the Jesuit college in Washington would alarm the American people, if they were not case-hardened and dead to reason. In one cellar beneath a Roman Catholic church is a cell in which is an iron cellar. It can be closed air-tight. What horrid crimes have been committed there, God only knows. Rome is not changed, in spirit or in purpose. She boasts of her intolerance, and practices her inhumanity whenever she can. Let a member of Congress determine, because of public opinion, and perhaps because of the intrinsic merits of a bill that obtains the approval of his judgment and because he believes it will advance the interests of his constituency to refuse a vote to advance a scheme upon which Rome has set its heart, or to pass an appropriation bill in which Rome has an interest, and *presto!* he finds himself antagonized by a spirit that infects the air and confronts and destroys his influence. An unseen hand is found directing affairs at the nominating convention and manipulating ballots at the polls. Because of this, the power of Rome is dreaded and courted in Washington and throughout the country.

ROME IS WELL SERVED.

Cardinal, archbishops, priests, brothers, monks, nuns, sisters of charity and of the poor—these, and an innumerable multitude beside, do her bidding. They will tell the truth, or a falsehood, in accordance with the needs of Rome. They will cringe and crawl as beggars, or frown and threaten as masters. They will deceive the very elect.

PAUL DESCRIBES THEM.

They are "lovers of their own selves, covetous, boasters, proud, blasphemers, disobedient to parents, unthankful, unholy, without natural affection, truce breakers, false accusers, incontinent, fierce, despisers of those that are good, traitors, heady, high minded, lovers of pleasure more than lovers of God; having a form of godliness and denying the power thereof. . . . For of this sort are they which creep into houses and lead captive silly women, laden with sins, led away with divers lusts, ever learning and never able to come to the knowledge of the truth; from such turn away."*

Beyond what are called the sacred orders, Rome has a vast constituency, which are being organized by the Jesuits into a great number of secret societies, the principal of which are: *"The Ancient Order of Hibernians" "Irish American* Society," *"Knights of St. Patrick," "Knights of the Red Branch"* etc., etc.; while it is said, and believed, there are 700,000 men enrolled under the name of U. S. Volunteers, Militia, and officered by some of the skillful generals and officers of the Republic. These are trained to antagonize the most sacred principles underlying the Constitution of the United States; such as, the equality of every citizen

---

* 2 Tim. 3:2-7.

before the law, liberty of conscience, independence of the civil from ecclesiastical power, freedom of worship, etc., etc.

The United States have established schools, where they invite the people to send their children, that they may cultivate their intelligence and become good and useful citizens. The church of Rome has publicly cursed all these schools and forbidden their children to attend them, under pain of excommunication in this world and damnation in the next. Not only does she antagonize our school system, claiming at the outset that it bore a religious character, because the Bible found in it a welcome; but having been the cause for banishing the Word of God, she pronounces the schools godless, and sends forth the decree to have all her children housed in the parochial school, and then, with an effrontery and inconsistency that is simply astounding, she seeks to officer the schools of Protestants, so that in some of the public schools in which there is hardly a single Roman Catholic child, and where there is a parochial school in the immediate neighborhood, Rome, through suffrage, obtains control of the School Board in our large cities, and then fills the schools with Roman Catholic teachers to instruct the children of Protestants. In one such school are forty-one teachers, thirty-nine of whom are Roman Catholics.

The Constitution of the United States finds in the people the source of civil power. Rome proclaims this principle impious and heretical, and claims that all governments must rest upon the foundations of the Catholic faith, with the Pope alone as the legitimate and infallible source and interpreter of the law. The Hon. Richard W. Thompson, late Secretary of the Navy, said: "Nothing is plainer than that, if the principles of the church of Rome prevail here, religious freedom is at an end. The two cannot exist together. They are in open and direct antagonism with the fundamental theory of our Government everywhere."

This statement would not convey any news to an intelligent and an instructed Romanist. The Roman Catholic Bishop Ryan, speaking in Philadelphia recently, said: "We maintain that the Church of Rome is intolerant; that is, that she uses every means in her power to root out heresy. But her intolerance is the result of her infallibility. She alone has the right to be intolerant, because she alone has the truth. The church tolerates heretics when she is obliged to do so; but she hates them with a deadly hatred, and uses all her power to annihilate them. If ever the Catholics should become a considerable majority, which in time will surely be the case, then will religious freedom in the Republic of the United States come to an end. Our enemies know how she treated heretics in the Middle Ages, and how she treats them to-day, where she has the power. We no more think of denying these historic facts, than we do of blaming the Holy God and the princes of the church for what they have thought fit to do."

This, though not a cheerful view, tells the truth, and prepares us, with renewed interest, to study the proofs, showing that Washington is in the lap of Rome, that we may better be prepared to understand the terrible tyranny there exercised, and the unscrupulous uses to which the results of this power is applied.

6

Rome In the Lap of Washington

NO SOONER HAD THE DISTRICT of Columbia been designated as the seat of the Capital of the United States, than Rome entered it, not as master, but as servant. Pius VII. had just reached the Papal chair, while the Continent about him was quaking beneath the resounding tread of Napoleon's embattled host. Romanism was having a hard struggle in Europe. She was not yet at home in America. She was on sufferance. Clement the Fourteenth had issued the bill abolishing the Society of Jesuits, just previous to the Declaration of Independence by the United States of America, saying, as he did so: "I sign my death-warrant; but I obey my conscience." "Watch the pot," became his watchword, as he dismissed one cook supposed to be under Jesuit control, and appointed another, a monk by the name of Francis, whom he thought he could trust.

The active prudence of the good monk did not disconcert the Jesuits; it only rendered them more ingenious in Europe, and coaxed them in great numbers to find a home and a theatre of operations in the regions beyond.

The following was the infernal trick they employed to attain their ends in Rome: "A lady of the Sabine, entirely devoted to them, had a tree in her garden which bore the handsomest figs in Rome. The reverend fathers, knowing that the Pope loved this fruit very much, induced the lady to disguise herself as a peasant, and go and present these figs to Brother Francis. The devotee did so several times, gained the confidence of the Franciscan, and one day slipped into the basket a fig larger than the others, into which a subtle poison, called *'aquetta,'* was injected. Up to this time the Holy Father had enjoyed perfect health; he was well made, though of the ordinary height; his voice was sonorous and strong; he walked with the activity of a young man, and everything presaged a long old age to him. From that day his health failed in an extraordinary manner; it was remarked with alarm that his voice was sensibly failing. To those first symptoms of his sickness was joined so violent an inflammation of his throat that he was obliged to keep his mouth constantly open; vomiting then succeeded the inflammation, accompanied by pains in his bowels; finally, the sickness increasing in its intensity, he discovered that he was poisoned. He wished to make use of antidotes, but it was too late; the evil was beyond remedy, and he had only to wait the close of his life. For the three months that he endured this terrible agony, his courage never failed him for a moment; one day only, after a more violent crisis than all the others, he said: "Alas! I knew well that they would poison me, but I did not expect to die in so slow and cruel a manner." Remember, a woman was the instrument of the Jesuits, as was Mary Surratt, a century later, in the taking off of the great Emancipator. The Pope was changed into a shadow. His flesh was eaten out by the corrosive action of the *"aquetta";* his very bones were attacked and became softened, contorting his members and giving them a hideous form. At last, worn out with suffering, the poor victim of the execrable Jesuits died, Sept. 22nd, 1774. Something of this was known by the builders of the Republic in America. In Assam missionaries are compelled to get accustomed to snakes. They climb up their door-jams; they find sleeping places in the roof and ceiling above them; they look down upon them, while they rest in bed. Sometimes a poisonous reptile is touched, and bites and kills. This is bad. Thousands of natives fall a prey to the reptiles, who live, and move, and have being in the country; yet, after all, missionaries get used to snakes. They learn to tolerate them. Some learn to pet them. They see natives who become snake-charmers, and boast of their ability; indeed, get their living by handling and sporting with snakes. The story is matched by the way Roman Catholics have come to be not only tolerated, but finally petted, courted, if not loved, in America. At the outset, the people felt a great repugnance towards them. The Christian people of the United States gave Roman Catholics a wide berth. The less they had of them the better. The story of the Inquisition was familiar. Washington dreaded foreign influence, und never saw but one Roman Catholic in whom he had comfort, the immortal Lafayette. Jefferson, Madison and others were afraid of the influence attempted to be exerted by the mischievous, persecuting, unreliable association known and designated as the Roman Catholic Church, which was to them *"The Wicked"*—*"The Mystery of Iniquity"*—"The Harlot of the Tiber"—The oppressor and inhuman foe of the Church of God in all ages and all climes. Hence Rome entered Washington, as elsewhere, as an object of dread. That College in Georgetown, District of Columbia, was regarded as a Jesuit nest. It was let alone by the North, and largely by the South. Then came the convent. Nuns began to appear. Their pious faces, demure appearance, deceived the very elect. The establishments they wanted for eleemosynary purposes, went up silently and almost unnoticed. Here was the Providence Hospital, corner Second and D streets. Beautiful name! All thought well of it. It was founded in 1802. That was in the midst of the war. The nuns wished to help nurse the wounded. "Why not let them? Who can do it better?" men said. The camel got his head in when hospital tents were whitening the hillsides and valleys of the land. Thaddeus Stevens asked and obtained an appropriation of $32,000 for the Providence Hospital. In 1864 it was incorporated. The Sisters of Charity were to have charge. The name "Sisters of Charity" sounds well. In 1867 the present building was commenced. It is now two hundred and eighty feet in length, built of brick, and will accommodate 250 patients, and the government supports seventy-five free beds.

Samuel J. Randall, the son of a Baptist, linked to the denomination by many enduring ties, married a wife in sympathy with Rome, gave his daughter to a Roman Catholic, and found in the hospital the best of care after those terrible nervous prostration attacks which come of too great mental strain when stimulus no longer furnishes relief. There he could go. All that love and care could do for him was done; all that political influence could do for them was done. And so appropriation after appropriation has been smuggled through; until, it is said and believed that, since 1866, over one million of dollars have been given by the nation to support Roman Catholic institutions in the City of Washington. This will be a surprise to many members of Congress now on duty. It will not be believed by some. Yet it is probably under, rather than over the truth. Rome builds her walls in troublous times. It was during the war that she appeared, the war in which she wrought as the traitor to liberty. She obtained a foothold from which it seems almost impossible to dislodge her. She came stealthily and unobtrusively: came as a helper by profession, as a flatterer by practice. Because women, dressed in the garb of nuns, came to strong men and asked for help, it was thought ungallant to deny them. They had been in the hospitals. The surgeons prized them. They gave no trouble. If things were wrong, they never made reports. Physicians and surgeons might be drunken and cruel, the Sisters of Charity gave no sign. The bad had all things in common. So they prospered there, and were rewarded when they needed help in Washington. Rome knows how to employ women in carrying forward her great schemes. Her history shows this.

ROME CAN BE SEEN AND STUDIED HERE.

In presenting Romish splendors and glories we are not compelled to cross the sea, to enter Italy, to pass through the gates of the seven-hilled city, to pass up the Appian or any other way; to enter St. Peter, or wander through the interminable passages and galleries of the Vatican. The Rome in which the Coliseum stands, and churches innumerable are found side by side with ruins sacred to memory and history, is not in our thought when it is declared that Rome found a place in the lap of Washington before Washington came to rest so quietly and contentedly in the lap of Rome. By Rome is meant, the spirit that distinguishes her, and the influences which gathered power in days that were dark and days that were bright. By Rome is meant, the men who serve at her altars; now known as a monk, then as a bishop, anon archbishop or a cardinal, but first and last as a Jesuit.

Lord Robert Montagu, formerly the companion of the Jesuits, says: "The system of the Church of Rome is a wonderful mechanism. Its centre is the Pope. Yet it is independent of the Pope. Many a Pope has been a dotard; very many have been debauchees; and still the machine works on, irrespective of his idiosyncracies. It is the Cabinet, the Privy

Council, the College of Cardinals that governs. That body never dies. One old man and another falls away, like a sere and yellow leaf; but the tree remains; the tradition and knowledge of centuries are still there. The records of the past are added to the daily experiences of the present; and that experience is being ever gathered in every corner of the earth, wherever there is a priest or a missioner. From every race, from every land, from every people, nay, from every family, there stretches a telegraphic wire of secret intelligence to the central section of the Vatican. There the intelligence is used by free minds, who are destitute of family, without all the affections that are natural to men; without a country or a home, without patriotism, without restraint of obligations, oaths, moral principles or divine laws; because the word of the Pope is supposed to tear those holy fetters away as gossamer webs; and priestly absolution is held to wash out even the slightest taint of sin."

"That is right which is done to advance the power of the Pope. That is true which the Pope may please to assert *ex cathedra*, that which favors the interests of the church is good. Even crime is commendable if it be done for the church. The advance of the Papacy has always been as the advance of the plague, irresistible, unsparing, remorseless, and deadly. Its myriads of secret agents overmatch armies and dispose of their generals. Its purposes are fathomless as the sea and silent as the grave: its action in every state, setting nation to hamper nation, and exciting one statesman against another; breaking up, dividing, crumbling its enemies, while its own party is always united; conspiring everywhere towards one object. Ever victorious, it will triumph, until the great hour for the doom of the harlot, which sits upon the nations of the earth, has struck, until the warning voice has been heard through the world, "Come out of her my people."

Having increased from 45,000 in 1783 in the United States, very largely through emigration and annexation; and having worked in accordance with one fixed and comprehensive plan, viz.: to get all possible in land, in influence, in gifts, and give out nothing and lose nothing,—having adopted a system of borrowing money by a kind of saving-bank process, illustrated by Archbishop Purcell of Cincinnati, whereby millions of dollars have been obtained and used for the purchase of real estate, building vast structures, and mortgaging them for all they can carry,—Rome has an appearance of prosperity, the result of dishonesty and deception, and entirely misleading. In Cincinnati and elsewhere, these vast sums used have been stolen from the poor, who have no redress except in suits of law, which are expensive, and which result in putting the litigant under the ban of the church.

The Pope claims that the church has an innate, legitimate right to the entire earth. Rome takes, holds, and uses property as if she were master. This property, to the extent of $300,000,000 in the U. S., is vested in the bishops. The people who give the money have no control of it. In England, Rome obtained possession, at one time, of *one-third* of the Kingdom; and it was only through the statute of mortmain deliverance was obtained. In Spain, in Mexico, in Italy, and in other Catholic countries, the civil power had to resort to confiscation, so that the people might have an opportunity to build; hence Church property should be taxed, and then Rome would be compelled to disgorge. The city of Brooklyn is robbed annually of $100,000 taxes on one piece of property captured by Jesuit cruelty and cunning, and yet there is not a church, nor an ecclesiastical edifice on it. The entire separation of church and state is the principle of our government, and to prevent the possibility of any sect, or combination of sects, from imposing, or even attempting to impose, a state church upon the United States, it was enacted March 4th, 1789, in the first amendment to the Constitution, that *"Congress shall make no law respecting an establishment of religion, or prohibiting the free exercise thereof,"* and yet public land and money has been given by the Government to the Roman Catholic church amounting to millions of dollars. The block on which the Fifth Avenue Cathedral stands in New York is valued at $4,000,000. Land has been given in many military posts for Roman Catholic chapels, in direct antagonism to the letter and spirit of the Republic.

This is the Rome that entered Washington, so soon as the wilderness began to bud and blossom towards its present life and state. Let us admit the truth. Rome has silently and stealthily coiled her folds about the capital, and few are aware of the peril which threatens the peace and prosperity of the nation.* Into Washington Rome came with exceeding care and grace. She has risen to power and dominion through the instigation of Satan and the instrumentality of designing men. Rome seeks political supremacy at the capital and throughout the nation. Is it not high time that every loyal citizen, and friend of religious and civil liberty, should awake to the importance of firmly withstanding the emissary in those places where she seeks control? No man who is a loyal Roman Catholic is properly qualified to be a representative in our national or state legislatures. No man who truckles to Romanism is fit to be a representative of a free people.

Let us not forget that the signal of our nationality was the signal of Rome's irrevocable decree to crush us in our might; and commencing with the honeyed expressions of the tongue and a sardonic smile upon her face, she has received largely and enjoyed long our national confidence and hospitality. We remembered that it was not the least of America's glory, that her Roman Catholic sons fought and suffered and perilled for her liberty; and we did not thus perceive that the Jesuitism, which then and now absolutely controls the church of Rome in the United States, never had anything in common with our institutions, the Declaration of Independence, or our Republican government. There is an eternal hostility between the principles of Washington and the principles of Popery, between the spirit of Romish priests and prelates and that of the fathers of the Republic, who owned allegiance only to God, and required no intercessor but His well-beloved Son. There were no surpliced traitors, no perfidious prelates, in that great convention which formed the eternal code of our liberties, and wrote our everlasting principles; but God-fearing, God-depending, God-trusting men of robust and manly life. It was no vulnerable conceited popinjay—but the spirit which had drawn lightning from the skies—who arose in that assembly, and to solve doubt, and difficulty, and danger said: "We seem to be at our wits' ends; we need help from above. *Let us pray.*" They knelt—the collected wisdom of America—before the God who had

---

* See Frontispiece.

given them Independence, that He might guide them to a Constitution wise and holy enough to save it. Let not their work be in vain. Put the trumpet to the lip, and sound the alarm: Papal Despotism has Washington in her grasp! The presence of the dragon is here and is felt; his breath is diffusing its poison; his touch has wounded, and already partially withered our schools, the ballot-box and the Bible. Men claiming to be Protestants are bartering the principles of American liberty for priestly influence and papal despotism. To head against it, *truth* must be told. Then will the clouds of mental and moral darkness be dissipated, and the poor, blinded Papists, in bondage to priestcraft, will come forth into the freedom of Bible and Republican independence.

The female Jesuit in America, as in Europe, is to be dreaded. No one can follow the trail of the Romish serpent without being convinced that Satan did not turn from women after he wrought the ruin of the father of the race through his seductive power over Eve. Through woman he finds a passage-way to the heart of man. No greater peril confronts us than is found in the readiness with which Protestant young men marry Roman Catholic wives. Gen. Wm. T. Sherman beclouded his life, gave up his hold upon the children God might give him, and so was robbed of his boy, and did injustice to his own high aims, when he took to his heart a woman who had first given herself to the priests of Rome. Because of this, he publicly declared he could not accept the nomination for the Presidency. Whatever he may do, or not do, she has been the willing and untiring servant of Rome. By her wiles another brilliant man lost the Presidency, and is to-day a broken wreck. There were good reasons why God forbade the children of Israel marrying wives from the heathen about them. When this was done, the woman captured the man and carried with her the children. Solomon, with all his wisdom, could not withstand her wiles. Rome understands this power, and places schools, filled with brilliant and captivating ladies, near the military posts, so as to capture the young men. Major-General Schofield was born into a Christian home, and had an honored father, who was a Baptist minister, but a Romish wife has taken him into the embrace of Rome. Let the warning be heeded. Judge Jesuitism by its infamous conduct towards the amiable Clement. Pius the Sixth came next. We cannot describe the plottings and conflicts which disturbed the church prior to his election. His character is made apparent by the utterance: *"Pius the Fifth is the last. .Pope canonized by the church, I wish to walk in his footsteps."* Pius the Fifth was the instigator of the St. Bartholomew massacre. Pius the Sixth has been described as enterprising and irresolute, interested and prodigal, suspicious and careless, false in heart and knavish in mind. Pius the Sixth had two children by his own sister!* His conduct infected Romanism. It was during his life as Pope, that Leopold of Tuscany, brother of Joseph Second of Austria, determined to clean out Tuscany by resisting the polluting tendencies of the Papacy. In "Why Priests Should Wed," there is no more terrible picture than is here set forth. Scipio di Ricci, through investigations, brought out revelations which horrified Europe. "From the declarations of the nuns, it was shown that in the convents of St. Lucia and St. Catherine at Pistoria, the female Dominicans received the confessors in the chapter and abandoned themselves to the most unbridled excesses of libertinage on the very steps of the altar; other nuns owned that frequently jealousy, or the inconstancy of the monks, led to serious collisions; that they disputed for the provincial, or prior; that they deprived themselves of their money or effects for their confessors; that several Dominicans had five or six mistresses at once, who formed a kind of seraglio; that at each promotion of a provincial in the monastery of the men, the newly chosen went to the convent to choose a favorite, and that the *novices, entirely naked, were ranged in two rows for his inspection; that he placed his hand on the head of her who pleased him most and made her his mistress at once."* Why are nunneries in Washington better than these pest houses? Has Rome changed? Scipio di Ricci, under the direction of Leopold, fought these enormities, and Pius the Sixth fought the Reformer and fulminated bull after bull against him. To clean out the impurities of the Papacy condemned the Pope of Rome.

---

* History of the Popes, by Louis Mare De Cormen, p. 398. *Ibid., p.* 403.

Then it was Voltaire led the philosophers in their attack upon the church. Free thought in Europe led to untrammeled thinking in the New World. Louis the Sixteenth expiated his crimes upon the scaffold. A Republic was proclaimed in France. It was the out frowth of the birth of the Republic of the United States. Pius the Sixth fulminates a bull of excommunication against the French nation, designating it by the names of "impious" "sacriligeous" and "abominable," and calls down upon it the thunders of heaven and earth. The Convention sends the following letter to His Holiness: "The Executive Council of the Republic to the prince bishop of Rome. Pontiff,—You will immediately discharge from your dungeons several French citizens who are detained in them. If these demands are ineffectual, you will learn that the Republic is too bold to overlook an outrage, or too powerful to allow it to go unpunished."

Then came the fight with Napoleon Bonaparte. Pius the Sixth endeavored to appease the storm; but these conflicts, and, above all, his debauchery with the beautiful Duchess de Broschi, his daughter, gave a fatal blow to his health. His two bastards, Romnald and the Duke de Broschi, hastened to lay hands on the treasures collected in the Vatican. Up rose the people against the Pontiff—kings informing him that he was no longer anything in the government. "And my dignity," exclaimed the Pope, anxiously; "what becomes of it?" "It will be preserved to you," said GeneralCervani; "and a provision of two thousand Roman crowns is granted you to maintain your rank." "And my person, what is to become of it?" "It is safe," replied Cervani; "and they will even grant you a hundred men for your guard." "I am still Pope, then," said the destroyer of his sister's virtue, with a strange laugh. Thus he went on, until the resources of life were used up by age, debaucheries, and excesses. A paralysis, which had at first fallen on his limbs, extended to his entrails, and freed the earth, on the 29th of August, 1799, of the last pontiff of the eighteenth century.

Then came Pius the Seventh. The new pope was elected after one hundred and four days of discussion and strife. To Napoleon he was indebted for his election. To Napoleon he became servile and fulsome, and exhausted all forms of adulatory thanks. He it was who left Rome and went to Paris to consecrate the Consul who had changed the Republic into an empire, and took to himself a crown. Pius the Seventh restored the Jesuits to power. He persecuted the good, and helped the bad; and on the 6th of July, 1822, fell in his chamber and broke his hip, and died April 20, 1823.

The Papacy, weak in Europe, was not strong in America. The Jesuits were alive there and here. They were hated there as here—they prospered there as here. Into Washington Rome came, not as a novice, but as an adept in the art of ruling. Everything was new and untried. Help was welcomed, come from whence it might. The Jesuits were wary and discreet. They represented an organization that joined together ancient civilizations. Truly has Macaulay said: "No other institution is left standing which carries the mind back to the times when the smoke of sacrifice rose from the Pantheon and when camel-leopards and tigers bounded in the Flavian amphitheatre. The proudest royal houses are but of yesterday, when compared with the line of supreme pontiffs. That line we trace back in an unbroken series from the Pope who crowned Napoleon in the Nineteenth century, to the Pope who crowned Pepin in the Eighth; and far beyond the time of Pepin the august dynasty extends, till it is lost in the twilight of fable."

Rome was full of life and vigor. Republics had been throttled in Europe. The attempt was to be made to destroy the one being established in America. There is much about Rome to give it prestige. Age does much. Pretension does more. She assumes apostolical pre-eminence. Few care to prove the falsity of the claims. They tolerate, they endure, and some embrace.

ROME POSES

as the sole authorized channel of Divine grace to saints and sinners. She has large endowments and accumulated wealth. She holds her church-edifices, monasteries, convents, educational and charitable establishments, by such a tenure as to be independent of contemporary fear or favor. By the skillful use of the political and social influence connected with its wealth and numbers and centralized organizations, it has facilities for advancing to honor, and otherwise repaying, those who sustain and honor her, and for hindering or preventing the prosperity of those who oppose her.

She has also an element of great strength in her grandeur and showy magnificence. Her grand cathedrals and churches, situated in the most desirable situations; her gorgeous ceremonies, and pompous processions, with all the adjuncts of unrivalled music and artistic splendor, produce their effect. Churches went up. They were beautiful to the eye. Priests walked in humility, not in pride. The war was no sooner over, than Rome built for the colored people the handsomest and most stately structure in Washington. That was smart. None knew it better than the priests of Rome. Pictures of the most costly character were hung on its walls. The altar drapery was of the best. White priests ministered at the altar; but schools were established for the education of black priests and black *nuns*. They call it St. Augustine. The name is good. The blacks and whites bow down together before false images and alike disobey God, and people call it "religion."

The Jesuits built St. Aloysius. In Washington all regard Jesuitism with favor. St. Matthew's is the home of diplomats. The great find there a welcome, and bow down to graven images. England disgraces herself and insults this country by sending a Roman Catholic as Minister to our Government; while she attempts to throttle the serpent seeking her life at home.

St. Patrick, on G and 10th Streets; Holy Trinity, Georgetown; Immaculate Conception, N and 8th Streets; St. Aloysius for the Jesuits, St. Augustine for the exclusive use of colored people; St. Dominic, E and 6th Streets; St. Joseph's; St. Mathew's, N and 15th Streets; St. Paul's, 15th and V; St. Peter's on Capitol Hill; St. Stephen's, Pennsylvania Ave. and 25th Street; St. Teresa's Anacosta; Visitation Convent Chapel, Tenallytown; St. Ann's, attended from Georgetown College. The descendants of Luther and Calvin came to America to have a church without a Pope, where they made a government without a throne. Will they fail?

That question must be answered by this generation. The conduct of the American people to-day is shaping the destiny of the nation's future. In the past, Rome has asked permission to exist. This request it was American to grant. To-day she demands the right to rule. This it will be American to repress.

7

The Hospitals Under Romish Control

IN ONE WAY OR ANOTHER Rome pushes her way to seats of power and influence. Is it because Protestants are too modest, or too indifferent, to resist? The Romish Priest is in the workhouse caring for paupers because Protestant ministers neglect to do it. He gets a chaplaincy in the prison and jail for the same reason. It is come to be believed that Roman Catholics are adapted to care for our eleemosynary institutions; such as hospitals, houses of refuge, orphan asylums and institutions of kindred character, as are not Protestants. Let us not find fault with Romanists for doing what Protestants neglect to do. Nothing could be more unfair or unwise. Let us not give over to Romanists work that we ought to do ourselves. It is a surprising fact, that every hospital in Washington is in the hands of Roman Catholics with one exception, and that has the treasurer and three members of the Board, Roman Catholics; that Sisters of Charity are the nurses; and that American citizens are compelled to see these representatives of a faith utterly distasteful to the majority enthroned in power.

As a rule, American citizens do not like the headgear of the "Sisters." "Why can't they take off those white-winged sun-bonnets in the ward?" asked one poor fellow, reared in a Protestant home, and yet sick in a hospital. "Sun-bonnets!" sneered another of the irreverent critics; "they're a cross between a white sun-bonnet and a broken down umbrella; and there's no name that describes them."*

This language describes the feeling of very many in the hospitals in Washington. They do not like the head-gear or the manners of the so-called "Sisters of Mercy." It is theory that there are no nobler and no

---

* Mary A. Livermore, in "The Story of the War," pp. 219.

more heroic women than those found in the Catholic sisterhoods. The fact explodes the theory. They are like other women: some are good, some are bad. Some kind, some cruel.

Rev. J. W. Parker, D.D., pastor, at one time, of the E-Street Baptist Church, of Washington, D.C., related, that his own brother was in a Washington hospital, and that nuns were the nurses. He desired a drink of water in the night, and asked for it, and overheard them say, "He is a heretic; let him choke."

A friend in such a hospital, with nuns as nurses, found herself in a constant worry, because she would keep her New Testament by her side, and would have her pastor visit her. The nuns did every disagreeable thing possible, until the minister told them that if such conduct did not cease, it would be reported at headquarters, and punishment would be demanded.

Another woman, who had been at one time a Roman Catholic, and who had been *converted* to Christianity, found herself in the hospital ministered unto by the Sisters of Mercy. They brought to her bedside a priest. She declined to see him. He persisted in coming. Her Protestant friends and the minister were told that she had gone back to the Church of Rome and that she did not wish them more. They believed the story, and stayed away for the time. They insisted on administering "extreme unction," daubed her with oil and drenched her with holy water, leaving her to die. The minister forced his way by the guards and got into the room.

"Why have you left me to the pitiless persecutions of these enemies of Christ?"

"They told me you wished it; that you had gone back to the idols of Rome, and turned your back on Christ." "It is a lie, a Popish lie; I have asked for you daily, I turned with loathing from their mummeries, but was compelled by weakness to endure this oil and holy water. Take me out of here."

The woman was removed to a home of love, where she was cared for. Why is such cruelty tolerated?

Clarence—was the brother of the architect who supervised the construction of a large addition to the most important public building in Washington. Clarence had won the heart of a daughter of a member of Lincoln's Cabinet. Her sister was married to an eminent lawyer, who was afterward a member of Garfield's Cabinet. The lady insisted upon a reformation of life, and his taking up and following some honest occupation. He accepted a position under his brother, but soon fell into his former ways. Worn out with a debauch which lasted several weeks, he entered the Providence Hospital, which deserves to be styled "The Drunkard's Retreat." Then he professed the Roman Catholic religion, without a reformation of life, and without giving up his cups even for a brief period, and in that faith lived and died a drunkard, and was buried in consecrated ground.

Another and a sadder scene. A lady, beautiful in face and form, was upon her death-bed. The priest came to administer extreme unction. He had, of course, the room to himself, and while with the lady alone, attempted an assault. She shrieked for help. The daughter, despite the rules of the church, burst into the room. "Turn the wretch out," exclaimed the mother, "and promise me, that come what will, you will never allow a priest to approach you, nor have more to do with the Church of Rome." The promise was made. Years passed. The daughter grew sick. Her friends were Roman Catholics. Her money was gone. She was compelled to be ministered unto by a Roman Catholic nurse, and because she would not suffer a priest to come and administer extreme unction, and die in the faith of Rome, they drew the bed from beneath her dying form, and left her upon the bare slats to lie, until a Protestant friend, now living in Washington, brought pillows and placed beneath her and took her to her own house, where she died. Then they would not let her rest, but dug up her body, carried it to consecrated ground, and boasted that she died in the Church of Rome.

Because such conduct is possible, Roman Catholic surgeons oppose the employment of Protestant nurses and declare they will not have them in the service, and that only the "Sisters" of the Catholic Church shall receive appointments. "I sought," said Mrs. M. A.

Livermore, "for the cause of this decision." "Your Protestant nurses are always finding some mare's nest or other," said one of the surgeons, that they can't let alone. They all write for the papers, and the story finds its way into print, and directly we are in hot water. Now, these "sisters" never see anything they ought not to see, nor hear anything, and they never write for the papers, and the result is, we get along very comfortably with them. It was futile to combat their prejudices, or to attempt to show them that they lacked the power to enforce their decisions."

Does not this explain why the "Sisters of Mercy" are preferred in Washington?

Here is a letter from a distinguished woman connected with a church of influence, and with societies which would gladly do the needed work. She writes:

"There is not a hospital in Washington where a Christian can go and feel that he or she is not confronted by Roman Catholics. Columbia Hospital for women, supported by Congress, has a drunken, brutal, Roman Catholic surgeon in charge. Priests are banqueted, and given full sway in the house; all the illegitimate children are christened by them, and the influence of Rome pervades every department. The hospital erected in memory of the sainted Garfield is infested by them, because of the idea, so prevalent, that Romanists are the only people who can do charity work. Alas for humanity, when such ideas prevail!"

Miss Mary A. Livermore, in her "Story of the War," speaks of the persistent effort to fill hospitals with "Sisters of Mercy," and exclude good, trained, excellent Protestant nurses. They would not be daunted or turned back. "Our husbands, sons and brothers need us and want us. If the surgeons are determined to employ Roman Catholic nurses, to the exclusion of Protestant, we shall contend for our rights, and appeal to the Secretary of War." They carried the day, and filled the land with their forces. Had the Protestant ladies of Washington manifested equal courage and persistency, they could have held control. The United States Hospitals got clear of the head-gear of the nuns, and filled their places with trained Protestant nurses.

On the tenth of June, 1861, Secretary Cameron vested Dorothea Dix with sole power to appoint women nurses in the hospitals. Secretary Stanton succeeding him, ratified their appointment. Miss Dix desired women over thirty years of age, plain almost to repulsion in dress, and devoid of personal attractions. Many of the women whom she rejected, because they were too young and too beautiful, entered the service under other auspices and became eminently useful. It is not necessary to have a nun's head-gear, nor a homely face, to make a woman a good nurse.

There was a time when the hospitals in Washington were marvels of order and comfort and neatness. Among the nurses were some of the very noblest women of the East. Women of culture, of family, and of rare nobleness of character acted as nurses. Too little praise has been bestowed upon the heroic Protestant nurses. Among the women famed in Washington was Miss Amy M. Bradley, an alert, executive woman from Maine. She had been a successful teacher before the war, and had already achieved an enviable reputation in the Hospital service of the Commission. For our men speedily fell victims to the malaria of the miasmatic swamps of the Chickahominy during the terrible Peninsular Campaign, in the spring and summer of 1862. The Hospital transports of the Commission did heroic service in those dark days, in removing the poor fellows North, where they could have a chance to live, or at least to die among their kindred.

Amy Bradley had made herself a power in these transports, by her skill in nursing, in preparing food for the sick and wounded, in dressing wounds, and in making herself generally useful to the wretched men temporarily placed under her care. She had charge of the Soldier's Home in Washington. Mrs. Livermore found it the abode of neatness and cheerfulness. The pleasant reading-room was filled with quiet readers, every man of whom seemed comfortable. As we spoke to them, each one had his grateful story to tell of Miss Bradley's care and faithfulness.

"Miss Bradley obtained over one hundred dollars' worth of back-pay for me, which I could not get myself," said one, "and I have forwarded it to my family, in need of it."

"One hundred dollars!" interjected another; "she has obtained over one hundred thousand dollars' worth of back-pay from the Government for soldiers since she came to the Home."

"She nursed over nine hundred of us, in the hospital," chimed in another; "and only thirteen died. Bring on your doctor who can do better."

"You ought to see the letters she writes every week for the men in the Home," added an assistant. "The letters she writes haven't any blue streaks in them, but are solid chunks of sunshine. Erect, decisive, quick of comprehension, and prompt in action, winning everyone by her kindly face, is it not strange that she was not given a place in one of the hospitals of Washington, and that they should all be surrendered to the representatives of the church of Rome?"

Permit Mrs. Livermore to describe another Protestant nurse.

"Among the hundreds of women who devoted a part, or the whole, of the years of the war to the care of the sick and wounded of the army, Mother Bickerdyke stands pre-eminent. She was unique in method, extraordinary in executive ability, enthusiastic in devotion, and indomitable in will. After her plans were formed and her purposes matured, she carried them through triumphantly, in the teeth of the most formidable opposition. She gave herself to the rank and file of the army,—the private soldiers,—for whom she had unbounded tenderness, and developed almost limitless resources of help and comfort. To them she was strength and sweetness, and for them she exercised sound practical sense, a ready wit, and a rare intelligence, that made her a power in the hospital or in the field. There was no peril she would not dare for a sick and wounded man, no official red tape of formality for which she cared more than a common tow-string, if it interfered with her work of relief. To their honor, be it said, the "boys" reciprocated her affection most heartily. "That homely figure, clad in calico, wrapped in a shawl, and surmounted with a 'shaker' bonnet, is more to this army than the Madonna to a Catholic," said an officer, pointing to her as she emerged from the Sanitary Commission headquarters, laden with supplies."

Mary A. Bickerdyke was born in Knox County, Ohio, July 19, 1817. She came of Revolutionary ancestors, and was never happier than when recounting the stories told her when a child by the grandfather who served with Washington during the seven years' struggle. Her husband died two years before the breaking out of the war. She was living in Galesburgh, Ill., and was a member of the Congregational Church when the war broke out. Hardly had the troops reached Cairo, when, from the sudden change in their habits, sickness broke out, and the ladies sent down Mother Bickerdyke. After the battle of Belmont she was appointed matron of the large post hospital at Cairo. The surgeon was given to drunkenness; he had filled all the positions in the hospitals with surgeons and officers of his sort, and bacchanalian carousals in the "doctor's room" were of frequent occurrence. "Sisters of Mercy" in that hospital would have been quiet. Soldiers might suffer. Officers and surgeons might drink to drunkenness, especially if they were Roman Catholics; but they would be mute and unobserving. They are this way in the hospitals in Washington, where drunken surgeons revel, priests christen their illegitimate children, while Government supports the concern, and all goes merry as a marriage bell.

Not so with Mother Bickerdyke. In twenty-four hours surgeon and matron were at swords' points. She denounced him to his face; and when the garments and delicacies sent her for the use of the sick and wounded disappeared mysteriously, she charged their theft upon him and his subordinates.

He ordered her out of the hospital, and threatened to put her out, if she did not hasten her departure. She replied that she would stay as long as the men needed her,—that if he put her out of one door she should come in at another. *When anybody left, it would be he, and not she.* She told him she had lodged complaints against him at headquarters. Finding a ward-master dressed in the shirt, slippers and socks that had been sent her for the sick, she seized him by the collar in his own ward, and disrobed him *"sans ceremonie"* before the patients. Leaving him nude, save his pantaloons, she uttered the parting injunction, "Now, you rascal, let's see what you'll steal next."

To ascertain who were the thieves of the food she prepared, she put tartar emetic in the peaches left on the table to cool. Then she went to her own room to await results. She did not have to wait long. Soon the sounds from the terribly sick thieves reached her ears, when, like a Nemesis, she stalked in among them. There they were, cooks, tablewaiters, stewards, ward-masters,—all save some of the surgeons—suffering terribly from the emetic; but more from the apprehension that they were poisoned.

"Peaches don't seem to agree with you, eh?" she said, looking at the pale, retching, groaning fellows, with a sardonic smile. "Well, let me tell you, that you will have a worse time than this, if you keep on stealing. You may eat something seasoned with rat-bane one of these nights." Colonel Grant was then in command. The thieves were returned to the regiments, honest men were substituted in their places, the drunken surgeon was removed, and one ing to an inner room; "but I guess he won't see you."

"Guess he will;" and she pushed into the apartment.

"Good morning General; I want to speak to you a moment. May I come in?"

"I should think you had got in," answered the General, barely looking up, in great annoyance. "What's up, now?"

"Why, General," said the earnest matron, in a perfect torrent of words, "we can't stand that last order of yours, no how. You'll have to change it, sure."

"Well, I'm busy to-day, and cannot attend to you. I will see you some other time." She saw the smile in the corner of his mouth, and replied: "General! don't send me away until you fix this." He fixed it, and for weeks all the sanitary stores sent from Nashville to Chattanooga, and the forts of that road, were sent, directly or indirectly, through this mediation of Mother Bickerdyke.

This woman, distinguished for common sense, for devotion to the soldiers, is left without employment, and nuns that never saw a battle-field, and Sisters of Charity that never had any sympathy with the soldiers, are placed in charge of Government hospitals, because

Protestants are dumb when they ought to speak, and blind when they ought to see.

This wonderful woman was for years without recognition from the Government, and is now in the pension office of San Francisco, when she belongs to the best hospital position in the gift of the Government. As when Moses and Aaron appeared before Pharaoh and used their wonder-working rod the magicians imitated them, so when the white wings of hospital tents were brightening the vision in various portions of the land Rome saw her opportunity and began her work in Washington.

The Providence General Hospital, corner of 2d and D streets, is famed in Washington. It was erected in the midst of the war.

Enter this hospital. Nuns have charge. The patients, be they Protestant or Roman Catholic, are expected to attend service in accordance with the forms of Rome. Proselyting is a business, and when this is impossible, the patient suffers.

Capt. Amos Cliff was in the Pension Bureau. He was sick. He carried to the hospital a watch and money, and after paying his board for a week, died. All his effects disappeared, as is the custom. The Grand Army Relief Committee, at the head of which is Capt. Frank A. Beuter, having learned of his death, went with Capt. D. A. Denison to inquire for him. No intelligence was furnished. He was a dead soldier. They knew where to look for his remains. His body was found in the Medical College, being cut up by the surgeons. The Grand Army boys took the mutilated remnants of a brave soldier, and, purchasing a coffin, sent what was left of an honored father to his friends. They who are so particular about giving a Roman Catholic burial, surrendered the body of a Grand Army soldier to the surgeon, not caring what was done with it or where it went, to a pauper's grave or a surgeon's table.

Imagine Mother Bickerdyke in such a position, and how different would be the treatment received!

It is fashionable to bow down to Rome. All seem aware that there are seven millions of Roman Catholics in this country. The many forget that *there are fifty millions who are not Roman Catholics,* who have some rights in this free land, which all are under some obligation to respect. The

Protestant element waits for a leadership. American citizens should be jealous of their rights. They should be, not only self-respecting, but self-asserting. God has planted, preserved and grown this nation, not to bow down to the worst despotism the world ever saw; but to lift up the enslaved, and cause them to read their possible destiny in the lines of promise written by God's providence in the marvellous possibilities placed within their reach. The Republic of the United States is to be the educator of the world. American citizens must keep this thought in mind, and so develop a higher type of humanity, better hospital service, a broader Christianity, and a nobler living than has hitherto blessed the world.

8

The Jesuits In Washington and Elsewhere

HOW ROME CREPT INTO WASHINGTON has been described. Stealthily, slowly, meekly, but surely, she came; and she came to stay. Long before the Revolution Rome was here. Washington saw her, and warned against her insidious influence. She came among us in poverty of spirit and in the ashes of humiliation. Anna Ella Carroll, of Maryland, a descendant of Charles Carroll of Carrollton, recited the story of Papal aggression, told of the holy confidence of the Pope, how the Jesuits determined "to convert every house in America into a fort, and to keep the gates open and the houses without defence." Protestants came and went freely, their honor, piety and loyalty to the Government was everywhere highly esteemed; and soon American Protestants placed their children in their hands for safe-keeping; helped them build their churches and public institutions because of their avowed purpose to enjoy our free institutions. They paraded in biblical plainness, and shut up the mystery of their pages from all sensitive readers. But while they wrote with a crow-quill for American liberty, they were making shoes to pinch the feet of the children whom they seduced to enter their schools, colleges and convents. They captivated women with little holy playthings, sympathized with their weaknesses, and ministered to their ills. They shut up the beautiful and innocent to make vows for Papal Jesuitism in free America. When they get the daughters, they want the sons, and in the name of liberty ask for the children. Their Propaganda of Rome, of Lyons, of France, of Vienna and Austria, build colleges, nunneries and monasteries, in which they offer education almost without money and without price, that they may stifle the hopes of the youth entrusted to their care.

Religious toleration has given welcome to a Jesuit priesthood that is making a religion without God and a state without liberty. They denounce the public schools, curse the Bible, murder history, and maim and mutilate literature. They teach American children, that all the founders of this Republic were Papists; that Washington, the father of his country, died a Roman Catholic, and in his last moments, it is asserted, confessed and communicated by the Romish Bishop of Baltimore; and that the relations of this great American patriot, fearing Americans would repudiate their hero, desired the secret never to be disclosed. The Romish community claim that they know of this conversion, and the Washington who wanted none but "Americans on guard," is a candidate for beatification by the Pope of Rome. Of course Columbus, the discoverer of America, was a Catholic. Lafayette, who came to our help, was brought here, it is claimed, through the interposition of Bishop Carroll, the Catholic, who in the interests of the Republic went to France to plead our cause. The best Republicans, they teach, are all Romanists. The writers of their school books exclude the history of distinguished Protestants, and fill their pages with the biographies of men and women who were loyal to Rome. This Papal influence came seeking little by little; it assumed, then boasted, and now denounces us. They say, Out of the church is no salvation. The monk says, Pray and read; while he stalks forth as though he had all America on a string of beads, carrying a pent-up fire to bum up the suspected and reviled intellects which come near him.

Jesuitism was born in Spain, reared in France, developed under Papal Rome, and diffused in the United States of America. The Company of Jesus, now in the United States, is great, powerful, and oppressive. It is mysterious and demoniacal, defying our science and weaving its malice over the brightest hopes of the world.

To describe Jesuitism, that was regarded as too foul and devilish to be borne even in Roman Catholic countries, seems to be a duty. Founded in 1534, and sanctioned by Pope Paul III. in 1540, it was expelled from England, 1581; France, 1594; Portugal, 1598; England again, 1604; France again, 1606; Russia, 1717; Portugal again, 1759;

France again, 1762-3; Spain, 1767; Genoa, 1767; Venice again, 1767; Sicily, 1767; Naples, 1768; Malta, 1768; Parma, 1768 ; all, with the exception of England and Russia, being strictly Roman Catholic states. Eventually, the Order was suppressed by Pope Clement XIV, in 1773; but continued to exist under other names, and disguised under the title of "Brothers of the Faith." It re-entered France, and had there several colleges in its hands, which were closed in 1828; some of them have since been reopened, and within the last twenty years, the number of persons belonging to the Order has been doubled. The Society was re-established by Pope Pius VII. in 1814, and finds free scope to carry out its treasonable designs under the American flag. Though it has stifled free thought wherever it could, introducing as their first injunction in all their schools, "Let no one, even in matters which are of no danger to piety, ever introduce a new question; "though it persecuted Galileo and oppressed Columbus; yet this Jesuit priesthood walks the soil of the Republic as a benefactor and finds in presidents and congressmen willing subjects of its will.

Henry IV. of France admitted to Sully, that he allowed the Jesuit priesthood to enter Catholic France only because he feared them! Philip II. of Spain, said: "The only Order of which I know nothing is the Jesuit." This, interwoven with Popery, is the Roman Catholic church of the United States. The federal compact, formed by the New England colonies in 1643, to resist the Indians, was the first Union made by the Anglo-Saxon upon our soil, and prepared the way for their Declaration of Rights later on. Jesuitism fought liberty amid its birth-throes. On the 10th of June, a resolution was adopted by a bare majority, and to obtain the unanimous sentiment of all the colonies a postponement was made until July, after securing the committee to draft the Declaration of Independence. Difficulties like mountains towered in the path of the Fathers. A spirit of opposition and discord pervaded their councils. They were driven to seek God's help. Congress paused to ask His guidance and blessing; and until He gave strength, union seemed impossible. The Committee reported on the twenty-eight of June, and on the 4th of July, 1776, by the final decision of Congress and the vote of every colony, this Declaration was engrossed; when, on the second of August, all the members present, and some who became so after the fourth of July, signed it in behalf of all the people. The bells then pealed the advent of Independence. But Romanists were then, as now, opposed to the upgoing structure. The Articles of Confederation and Perpetual Union between the thirteen original States were not ratified until 1781, because the Roman Catholics of Maryland opposed and refused to unite; so steadfast has ever been the opposition of the Romish priesthood to our liberty.

Attention has recently been turned to where the Jesuits are at work and what they are doing.*

"In the Balkan Peninsula there are forty-five Jesuit missionaries; in Africa, and especially Egypt, Madagascar, and the Zambesi region, 223; in Asia, especially Armenia, Syria, and certain parts of China, 699. In China alone the number is 195—all of French nationality. In Oceanica, including the Philippines, the Malay Archipelago, Australia, and New Zealand, the number is 270; in America, including certain specified States of the Union, portions of Canada, British Honduras, Brazil and Peru, 1,130; the total number of Jesuits scattered over the Globe, in purely missionary work, being 2,377. These are of various nationalities: but the vast majority are French. In the distribution great attention is paid to nationality; thus in Illyria, Dalmatia, and Albania, they are all Venetians; in Constantinople and Syria, Sicilians; in Africa, Asia Minor and China, French; while no French Jesuits are to be found in any part of the American Continent. In the Bombay and Bengal Presidencies, they are Germans and Belgiums, respectively; in the Philippines, Spanish; in the Malay Archipelago, Dutch; in Eastern Australia and New Zealand, Irish; in the United States, Germans, Neapolitans, and Piedmontese, are found working in specified and distinct districts; those laboring among the Indians of Canada are Canadians; in the British West India Colonies, they are English; in Central America, Spaniards; in South America, Italians, Spaniards and Germans, the Italians and Germans having all Brazil to themselves, doubtless because of the

---

* Etudes Religeuse.

enormous Italian and German immigration to Brazil. It will be understood that the spheres of labor of the different orders, are carefully laid down at Rome."

During the war, Washington saw the peril. While the American Revolution was progressing, our Continental Congress forbade any but her native sons to be employed in the foreign service of the country. Said George Washington: "You are not to enlist any person suspected of being an enemy to the liberty of America." One hundred chosen men were to be enrolled to form a corps to be instructed in the manoeuvres necessary to be introduced into the army, and serve as models for the execution of them. "They *must be American-born.*" "*Put none but Americans on guard*" came, because of the fear of foreign influence. "I do most devoutly wish that we had not a single foreigner amongst us, except the Marquis de Lafayette."* Thomas Jefferson recommended to the Postmaster General "to employ no foreigner, or revolutionary tory, in any of his offices." This was in the olden time. Notwithstanding this, concession followed concession, until the offices of the land were filled with foreigners, and American-born citizens were at a discount. Said Archbishop Hughes: "Irishmen in America are learning to bide their time. Year by year the Irish are becoming more and more powerful in America. At length the propitious time will come—some accidental, sudden collision, and a Presidential campaign at hand. *We will then use the very profligacy of our politicians for our purposes.* They will want to buy the Irish vote, and we will tell them how they can buy it, in a lump, from Maine to California."†

At present, Washington is in the toils of Rome. The serpent has entwined its folds about the Capitol, and all who would have honor, peace or promotion must bend the neck. It was in 1855 a writer declared, that "the National Administration was in the hands of a foreign, Roman-Catholic hierarchy. The Postmaster General was an Irish Roman Catholic at the dictation of the Pope of Rome, to obtain

---

* Letter to Governor Morris, White Plains, July 24, 1778, by Geo. Washington.
† Pp. 352.

direct access to the postal concerns and dearest rights of the American people."

In the State Department at Washington, not only a majority of the subordinates were foreign Roman Catholics, but they occupied the most important posts in the trust and confidence of the American Government. "Are you a Roman Catholic foreigner?" is the question put to the applicant, and, if answered in the affirmative, the sons of Revolutionary officers, who gave their houses to the flames and their bodies to the bayonet, are indecently thrust aside. Our naturalization laws are evaded—criminals and paupers vote down Americans at the ballot-box. Public and free schools are antagonized, the Bible driven out, expelled and burned. The police of our large cities are largely foreigners; while at one time thirty-nine on the police force of New York were branded as criminals from the prisons of Europe. These are the hordes which rush to our shores for democratic liberty, and have imposed upon them by the Jesuit masters the obligation to go *armed* to the ballot-box, and vote for Rome at the dictation of the Pope, and against liberty—against the public school, and the best interests of their adopted country.

At least four-fifths of these aliens come to our shores to escape the persecution of the Papal despots at home, and to find refreshment in pastures green beyond the sea. These fill our poor-houses, our jails, prisons, and lunatic asylums; and why not? Jail birds are promised liberty if they will emigrate to America. In 1837 the Mayor of Baltimore detected a shipload of 260 persons, at Fort McHenry, who as criminals were brought into port in irons. The Mayor remonstrated, and asked Martin Van Buren to order them back; but he replied, that there was no power to prevent their landing, and so these miserable wretches were permitted to join the party that flattered the Rebellion and attempted to break up the union of States by breaking up the union of hearts. Throughout Germany, as throughout Ireland, agents in the pay of steamship lines, who desired freight, advised the maimed, deformed, and crippled to take passage to Baltimore, New Orleans and Quebec, instead of New York, because in those places no laws exist to prevent their landing. Father Chiniquy relates, in his "Fifty Years in the Church of Rome," these facts (pp 668-687):

"It was in the spring of 1852, a large assembly, composed principally of priests, met at Buffalo, to confer with D'Arcy McGee, then editor of the *Freeman's Journal,* in regard to peopling the prairies of the West with Irish Roman Catholics. He published several able articles to show that the Irish people, with very few exceptions, were demoralized, degraded, and kept poor, around their groggeries, and showed how they would thrive, become respectable and rich, if they could be induced to exchange their grog-shops for the fertile lands of the West. A large assembly gathered. Great was the disappointment of D'Arcy McGee when he saw that the greatest part of those priests were sent by the bishops of the United States to oppose and defeat his plans.

"He vainly spoke, with burning eloquence, for his pet scheme. The majority coldly answered him: 'We are determined, like you, to take possession of the United States, and rule them; but we cannot do that without acting secretly, and with the utmost wisdom. If our plans are known, they will surely be defeated. What does a skillful general do when he wants to conquer a country? Does he scatter his soldiers over the farm-lands, and spend their time and energy in ploughing the fields and sowing grain. No! He keeps them well united around his banners, and marches at their head to the conquest of the strongholds, the rich and powerful cities. The farming countries then submit, and become the price of his victory, without moving a finger to subdue them. So it is with us. Silently and patiently, we must mass our Roman Catholics in the great cities of the United States, remembering that the vote of a poor journeyman, though he be covered with rags, has as much weight in the scale of power as the Millionaire Astor, and if we have two votes against his one, he will become as powerless as an oyster. Let us then multiply our votes; let us call our poor but faithful Irish Catholics from every corner of the world, and gather them into the very hearts of those proud citadels which the Yankees are so rapidly building under the names of Washington, New York, Boston, Chicago, Buffalo, Albany, Troy, Cinncinnati, St. Louis, Kansas City, San Francisco, etc. Under the shadows of those great cities, the Americans consider themselves as a giant and unconquerable race. They look upon the poor Irish Catholic people with supreme contempt, as only fit to dig their canals, sweep their streets, and work in their kitchens. Let no one awake those sleeping lions, to-day. Let us pray God that they may sleep and dream their sweet dreams a few years more. How sad will be their awakening, when, with outnumbering votes, we will turn them out forever from every position of honor, power and profit! What will those hypocritical and godless sons and daughters of the fanatical Pilgrim Fathers say, when not a single judge, not a single teacher, not a single policeman will be elected if he be not a devoted Roman Catholic? What will those so-called giants think of our matchless shrewdness and ability, when not a single senator or member of Congress will be chosen, if he be not submitted to our holy father the Pope? What a sad figure those Protestant Yankees will cut when we will not only elect the President, but fill and command the armies, man the navies, and hold the keys of the public treasury! It will then be time for our faithful Irish people to give up their grog-shops, in order to become the judges and governors of the land. Then our poor and humble mechanics will leave their damp ditches and muddy streets, to rule the cities in all their departments, from the stately mansion of Mayor of New York, to the humble, though not less noble, position of teacher.

"Then, yes! then, we will rule the United States, and lay them at the feet of the Vicar of Jesus Christ, that he may put an end to their godless system of education, and sweep away those impious laws of liberty of conscience, which are an insult to God and man! D'Arcy McGee was left almost alone when the votes were taken. From that time the Catholic bishops and priests have gathered their legions into the great cities of the United States, and the American people must be blind indeed, if they do not see that, if they do nothing to prevent it, the day is very near when the Jesuits will rule this country, from the magnificent White House at Washington, to the humblest civil and military department of this vast Republic. They are already the masters of New York, Baltimore, Chicago, St. Paul, New Orleans, Mobile, Savannah,

Cincinnati, Albany, Troy, Buffalo, Cleveland, Milwaukee, St. Louis, San Francisco. Yes! San Francisco, the great queen of the Pacific, is in the hands of the Jesuits.

"From the very first days of the discovery of the gold mines of California, the Jesuits had the hope of becoming masters of these inexhaustible treasures, and they secretly laid their plans with the most profound ability and success. They saw at once that the great majority of the lucky miners, of every creed and nation, were going back home as soon as they had enough to secure an honorable competence to their families. The Jesuits saw at a glance that if they could persuade the Irish Catholics to settle and remain there, they would soon be masters and rulers of that Golden City, whose future is so bright, so great! And the scheme, worked day and night with the utmost perseverance, has been crowned with perfect success. The consequence is, that while you find only a few American, German, Scotch and English millionaires in San Fransisco, you find more than fifty Irish Catholic millionaires in that city. Its richest bank (Nevada Bank) is in their hands, and so are all the street railways. The principal offices of the city are filled with Irish Roman Catholics. Almost all the police are composed of the same class, as well as the volunteer military organizations. Their compact unity in the hands of the Jesuits, with their enormous wealth, make them almost supreme masters of the mines of California and Nevada.

When one knows the absolute, abject submission of the Irish Roman Catholics, rich or poor, to their priests,—how the mind, the soul, the will, the conscience, are firmly and irrevocably tied to the feet of the priests,—he can easily understand that the Jesuits of the United States form one of the richest and most powerful corporations the world ever saw. "It is well known that fifty Catholic millionaires, with their myriads of employees, are, through their wives and by themselves, continually at the feet of the Jesuits, who swim in a golden sea." No one, if he be not a Roman Catholic, or one of those so-called Protestants who give their daughters to the nuns and their sons to the Jesuits to be educated, has much hope, when the Jesuits rule, of having a lucrative office in the United States, to-day. It is to San Francisco that you must go to have an idea of the number of secret and powerful organizations with which the Church of Rome prepares herself for the impending conflict, through which she hopes to destroy the schools, and every vestige of human rights and liberties in the United States. Washington is the nerve-centre of the organism. Baltimore is the city in which the machinery of Rome lies concealed. If it is true that from this centre the war was planned to disrupt the Union, it ought to be known.

The Jesuits are a *military organization,* not a religious order. Their chief is a general of an army, not the mere father-abbot of a monastery. And the aim of this organization is *Power*—power in the most despotic exercise; absolute power, universal power, power to control the world by the volition of a single man. Jesuitism is the most absolute of despotisms, and at the same time, the greatest and the most enormous of abuses. The General of the Jesuits insists on being master, sovereign over the sovereign. Wherever the Jesuits are admitted they will be masters, cost what it may. Their Society is by nature dictatorial; and, therefore, it is the irreconcilable enemy of all constituted authority. Every act, every crime, however atrocious, is a meritorious work, if committed for the interest of the Society of the Jesuits, or by the order of its General.

In the allocution of September, 1851, Pius IX. said: "That he had taken this principle for a basis,

That the Catholic religion, *with all its votes, ought to be exclusively dominant in such sort, so* that *every other worship shall be banished and interdicted."* "You ask, if the Pope were lord of this land and you were in a minority, what he would do to you? That, we say, would entirely depend upon circumstances. If it would benefit the cause of Catholicism, he would tolerate you; if expedient, he would *imprison or banish you, probably he might hang you.* But be assured of one thing, he would never tolerate you for the sake of your glorious principles of civil and religious liberty."

The *Rambler,* one of the most prominent Catholic papers of England, Sept. 1851, says: "Without Romanism, the last awful civil war would have been impossible. The South would never have dared attack the North, had they not had the assurance from the Pope that the

Jesuits, the bishops, the priests, and the whole people of the Church of Rome would help them. Because of this, the Roman Catholic Beaureguard was chosen to fire the first gun at Sumter. The Pope of Rome was the only crowned prince in the whole world who recognized the Southern Confederacy, and the pirate ship Alabama was commanded by Admiral Semmes, a Roman Catholic. Rome has not changed. The enemy of liberty before the war, it seems inexplicable that the defenders of liberty, and the victorious champions of freedom, should so far forget history, and so utterly ignore the rights of the Republic, as to play into the hands of Rome, the eternal foe of the principles embodied in the Republic.

"Another fact, to which the American Protestants do not sufficiently pay attention is, that the Jesuits have been shrewd enough to have a vast majority of Roman Catholic generals and officers to command the army and man the navy of the United States."

"Rome is a constant conspiracy against the rights and liberties of man all over the world; but she is particularly so in the United States. The laws of the church of Rome are in absolute antagonism to the laws and principles which are the foundation stones of the Constitution of the United States."

The United States affirm the equality of all citizens before the law. Rome denies it. Liberty of conscience is proclaimed by the United States. Rome declares it to be a godless, unholy, and diabolical thing. Separation of Church and State *is* an American doctrine. Rome is for the union. The State is but the annex. The church is all in all.

The Constitution of the United States fights persecution for opinion's sake; Rome champions it.

The United States seeks, through the public school, to secure the education of all the children. Rome curses the public schools, and seeks to supplant them with others in which Romanism shall be taught.

The United States recognizes in the people the primary source of civil power. Rome proclaims this principle heretical and impious. She says that "all government must rest upon the foundation of the Catholic faith, with the Pope alone as the legitimate and infallible source and interpreter of the law."

All this shows that Rome is the absolute and irreconcilable foe of the United States. Being entrenched in Washington and feared there, it is feared throughout the Republic. Beaten there, its defeat will not be difficult elsewhere.

9

Romanism the Assassin of Abraham Lincoln

THE CHARGE THAT ROMANISM was the assassin of Abraham Lincoln was first brought to the attention of the American people by Rev. Charles Chiniquy in his "Fifty Years in the Church of Rome." The proofs are there. Rome has answered the charges in the old way, by fire. Again and again have her minions tried to destroy man, book, and plates by burning the place where the book was printed and stored. Over and over again they have tried to kill the great apostle, but he still survives, and the light he kindled is shedding its glad radiance upon the world.

In 1851 he removed with a colony to St. Anne, Illinois, to begin the cultivating of the prairies of the West with Roman Catholics. His experience there was terribly sad. Born in Kamoraska, Canada, July 30, 1809, converted to Christ by reading the Scriptures when but a child, as a priest his life shows that a pure man in the Church of Rome has a hard time. No sooner had he begun his life in Illinois than he found a dissolute priesthood in antagonism to him and his work. They plotted against his reputation, and charged him with crimes which, if not disproved, would have incarcerated him in the State penitentiary for life.

It was then he turned to Abraham Lincoln, who, first as a lawyer and afterwards as a friend, served him with matchless ability. Because of this, when Mr. Lincoln became President of the United States, and was threatened by Romish priests with assassination, Father Chiniquy came to Washington to warn him of his peril, and give him proof of a friendship that through years remained unchanged. As an evidence of their close intimacy turn back a little. We are in Urbana, Illinois. Behold Abraham Lincoln as the champion of the betrayed priest.

A priest had accused Father Chiniquy of assaulting a woman, and had offered to give one of his dupes a large sum for swearing to the charge. Twelve men had proven the accuser to be a drunkard and a disreputable man; and yet it seemed impossible to secure any testimony that would disprove the charge.

Said Abraham Lincoln: "There is not the least doubt in my mind that every word this priest has said is a sworn lie; but the jury think differently. The only way to be sure of a verdict in your favor is, that God Almighty would take our part and show your innocence. Go to him and pray, for he alone can save you."

All that night he spent in prayer; at three o'clock in the morning he heard knocks at the door. On opening it, he saw Abraham Lincoln with a face beaming with joy. The story of the trial had been published in the Chicago papers. His condemnation was prophesied.

Among those who bought the papers was a man named Terrien. He read the story to his wife. She was much affected, and declared that it was a plot against a true man, saying: "I was there when the priest, Le Belle, promised his sister 160 acres of land if she would swear to a false oath and accuse Chiniquy of a crime which he had not even thought of, with her."

"If it be so," said Terrien, "we must not allow Father Chiniquy to be condemned. Come with me to Urbana." Being unwell, Mrs. Terrien said: "I cannot go; but Miss Philomene Moffat was with me then, she knows every particular of the wicked plot as well as I do. She is well, take her to Urbana."

This was done, and Father Chiniquy was saved. The joy of his deliverance was mixed with sorrow, because of what he feared his deliverance would cost his friend. Tears ran down his face. "Why weep?" asked Abraham Lincoln. "Because," said Father Chiniquy, "of what it may cost you." There were ten or twelve Jesuits in the crowd who had come from Chicago and St. Louis to see me condemned to the penitentiary, but it is on their heads you have brought the thunders of heaven and earth; nothing can be compared to the expression of their rage against you, when you not only wrenched me from their cruel hands, but made the walls of the court-house tremble under the awful and superhumanly eloquent denunciation of their infamy, diabolical malice, and total want of Christian and humane principle in the plot they had formed for my destruction. What troubles my soul just now and draws my tears is, that it seems to me I have read your sentence of death in their bloody eyes. How many other noble victims have fallen at their feet. He tried to divert my mind; then became more solemn, and said: 'I know the Jesuits never forget nor forsake. But man must not care how or when he dies at the post of honor or duty.'"

A few years pass. Abraham Lincoln is President of the United States. On his way to Washington a Roman-Catholic plot to assassinate him was frustrated by his passing *incog.* a few hours before they expected him. In August, another plot was concocted; which, coming to the ears of Father Chiniquy, caused him to go to Washington. The story of his experience and the relation of what the President said to him is of thrilling interest.

President Lincoln then told him: "We have the proof that the company which had been selected and organized to murder me was led by a rabid Roman Catholic named Byrne; it was almost entirely composed of Roman Catholics. More than that, there were two disguised priests among them to lead and encourage them. Professor Morse, the learned inventor of electric telegraphy, tells me that recently, when he was in Rome, he found the proofs of a most formidable conspiracy against this country and all its institutions. It is evident that it is to the intrigues and emissaries of the Pope we owe, in great part, the horrible civil war which is threatening to cover the country with blood and ruin."

Mr. Lincoln had been astonished by the statement published in the Roman Catholic papers that he had been born into the Roman Catholic church and had been baptized by a priest. They called him a renegade and an apostate on account of that, and heaped upon his head mountains of abuse.

"At first," said Mr. Lincoln, "I laughed at that, for it is a lie. Thanks be to God, I have never been a Roman Catholic. No priest of Rome has ever had his hand upon my head. But the persistency of the Romish press to present this falsehood to their readers as a gospel truth must have a meaning. What is it?"

"It was this story," said Father Chiniquy, "that brought me to Washington. It means your death. It is told to excite the fanaticism of the Roman Catholics to murder you. In the church of Rome an apostate is an outcast who has no place in society and no right to live. The Jesuits want the Roman Catholics to believe that you are a monster, an enemy of God and of his church; that you are an excommunicated man. Gregory VII. decreed that the killing of an apostate is not murder, but a good Christian act. That decree is incorporated in the canon law which every priest must study, and which every good Catholic must follow. My dear Mr. President, my fear is that you will fall under the blows of a Jesuit assassin, if you do not pay more attention than you have done up to the present time to protect yourself. Remember, because Coligny was a Protestant, he was brutally murdered on St. Bartholomew's night; that Henry IV. was stabbed by the Jesuit assassin, Revaillac, the 14th of May, 1610, for having given liberty of conscience to his people; and that William, Prince of Orange, the head of the Dutch Republic, was stricken down July 10th, 1584, by Girard, the fiendish embodiment of all that was crafty, bigoted, and revengeful in Spanish Popery. The church of Rome is absolutely the same to-day as she was then; she does believe and teach to-day as then, that it is her duty to punish by death any heretic who is in her way, or an obstacle to her designs.

"My blood chills in my veins when I contemplate the day which may come, sooner or later, when Rome will add to all her iniquities the murder of Abraham Lincoln."

"Yes," said Abraham Lincoln, "Professor Morse has already opened mine eyes to this subject. He has truly said: 'Popery is apolitical system; despotic in its organization, anti-democratic and anti-republican, and cannot therefore exist with American republicanism.'

"The ratio of the increase of Popery is the exact ratio of the decrease of civil liberty.

"The dominion of Popery in the United States is the certain destruction of our free institutions." "Popery, by its organization, is wholly under the control of a foreign, despotic Sovereign." "Popery is a union of Church and State; nor can Popery exist in this country in that plenitude of power which it claims as a divine right, and which in the very nature of the system it must continually strive to obtain, until such a union is consummated. Popery is, therefore, destructive to our religious and civil liberty."

"Popery is more dangerous and more formidable than any power in the United States, on the ground that, through its despotic organization, it can concentrate its efforts for any purpose with complete effect; and that organization being wholly under foreign control, it can have no real sympathy with anything American. Popery does not acknowledge the right of the people to govern, but claims for itself the supreme right to govern people and rulers by divine right. Popery does not tolerate the liberty of the press. It takes advantage, indeed, of our liberty of the press to use its own press against our liberty; but it proclaims in the thunders of the Vatican, and with a voice which it pronounces unchangeable, that it is a liberty never sufficiently to be execrated and detested. It does not tolerate liberty of conscience or liberty of opinion. They are denounced by the Sovereign Pontiff as a most pestilential error, a pest of all others to be dreaded in the State. It is not responsible to the people in its financial matters. It taxes at will, and is accountable to none but itself."[*]

These utterances were based on undisputed facts. Abraham Lincoln believed them, hence he said: "If the Protestants of the North and the South could learn what the priests, nuns, and monks, who daily land on our shores, under the pretext of preaching their religion, were doing in our schools and hospitals, as emissaries of the Pope and the other despots of Europe, to undermine our institutions and alienate the hearts of our people from our Constitution and our laws, and prepare a reign of anarchy here, as they have done in Ireland, in Mexico, in Spain, and wherever there are people that wish to be free, they would unite in taking power out of their hands."

---

[*] Foreign Conspiracy of the United States, by S. F. B. Morse, p. 129.

If Abraham Lincoln had said this to the American people rather than to an individual, they would have taken this power out of the hands of Rome, and buried slavery and Romanism in a common grave.

It is now known that the conspirators against liberty relied upon the support of Romanists in the North and in the South. But when the echoes of the guns of Sumter flew over the land, it called into active life the slumbering patriotism of a great people; the tide swept everything before it; the people would brook no opposition. Romish priests and people bowed to the supremacy of the patriotic sentiment. Flags were unfurled from church-spire and from house-top. No Romish conspirator in the great cities of the North dared show his hand; the people ran away from their priests; their conduct was a revelation. It showed to papal emissaries that a people who had fled Europe because of despotism, were not ready to betray liberty in America, the land of the free. Hence Romanists who had enjoyed the blessings of liberty enrolled themselves under the star-spangled banner, and went trooping off to the war for the Union. Romish priests were taken by surprise; they bent before the swelling current. Flags floated from cathedral spires and parish steeples until Rome was heard from, and then flags were pulled down, lest their church should ignore its sacred calling. They forgot that the Pope lived in Rome because of the help, not of spiritual power, but of the support of French bayonets; that in St. Louis, Mo., when the great cathedral was dedicated, the host was elevated to the music of belching cannon, flags were unfurled and lowered before the wafer-God of Rome, and that soldiers with drawn swords stood on each side of the high altar during service, claiming that in Roman Catholic St. Louis, or in Spain, the military is recognized as the right arm of the church.

Romanism opposed the North because Romanism is the foe of liberty. Romanism encouraged the South because the corner-stone of the Southern Confederacy rested upon human slavery. How the colored people of the South or the North can forget this and unite with the Roman Catholic church is a mystery. It is the theory of Rome that the toilers should be kept in ignorance. Gentlemen for the palace and serfs for the field, is the spirit of Romanism, incarnated in every despotic government where its power is supreme.

Louis Napoleon, the ally of Pius IX., expected to build up in Mexico a Roman Catholic kingdom, and unite it with the Southern States, and so establish a Latin Empire in the new world.

The Emancipation Proclamation spoilt the programme. How strange, how inexplicable are events, when studied in the light of an over-ruling Providence! For months, Abraham Lincoln had a vow registered before Almighty God to issue the Emancipation Proclamation, and give freedom to the negro, providing a victory was won at Antietam. The victory came. But Wm. H. Seward and S. P. Chase objected to the issuance of the Proclamation at a time of general depression in military affairs. The President waited until he could wait no longer. He called a Cabinet meeting, read his paper, and declared his purpose to send it forth. Suggestions were made. Some were received, some were rejected. The Proclamation went forth, and winged its way over the world. It reached France at the time when Louis Napoleon had proposed, and was about sending forth a letter recognizing the Southern Confederacy.

That morning the Proclamation of Liberty appeared. Paris was ablaze with excitement. Vivas of liberty filled the air, and Napoleon, knowing that a recognition of the Southern Confederacy was impossible, Maximillian was surrendered to his fate, and the dream of a monarchy in Mexico was exploded.

THE POPE HAD LESS SENSE.

Claiming that Abraham Lincoln was an apostate, the plot was laid to destroy him. On Dec. 3rd, 1863, Pius IX. uncovered his hand and heart in his letter to Jefferson Davis. That letter, after all that Abraham Lincoln had borne and was bearing for the brotherhood of man, was a severe sword-thrust at his heart and hope.

Hear Pius IX. to Jefferson Davis:

"Illustrious and Honorable President:—We have just received, with all suitable welcome, the persons sent by you to place in our hands your letter, dated the 23rd of September last."

He then takes ground, not for liberty, not for the deliverance of 4,000,000 bondsmen from the hell of human slavery, but for peace; which meant, building up the Confederacy on slavery as a corner-stone.

He added these words:

"We, at the same time, beseech the God of mercy and pity to shed abroad upon you the light of his grace, and attach you to us by a perfect friendship."

"Given at Rome at St. Peter's, the 3rd day of December, 1863, of our Pontificate, 18. Pius IX."

This letter came like a clap of thunder in a clear sky. Let us keep a few dates in mind. The Emancipation Proclamation was issued Sept. 22, 1862. This was followed by another, issued Jan. 1st, 1863, giving freedom to all slaves, and also that such persons of suitable condition would be received into the armed service of the United States, to garrison forts, and man vessels of all sorts in said service. And upon this, sincerely believed to be an act of justice, warranted by the Constitution, upon military necessity, "I invoke the considerate judgment of mankind, and the gracious favor of Almighty God."

Deliberately and ostentatiously, the Pope on the December following recognizes the Southern Confederacy, sides with despotism against liberty, and takes under his protection the chief conspirator against the Republic of the United States!

"Have you read the Pope's letter?" said Abraham Lincoln to Father Chiniquy, "and what do you think of it?" (p. 701).

"That letter is a poisoned arrow thrown by the Pope at you personally, and it will be more than a miracle if it be not your irrevocable death-warrant.

"That letter tells logically the Roman Catholics, that you, Abraham Lincoln, are a bloody tyrant, a most execrable being, when fighting against a government which the infallible and holy Pope recognizes as legitimate."

In reply, Mr. Lincoln spoke with great feeling, saying: "You confirm me in the views I had taken of this letter of the Pope. Prof. Morse is of the same mind with you. It is indeed the most perfidious act which could occur under the present circumstances. You are perfectly correct when you say that it was designed to detach the Roman Catholics who had enrolled in our armies. Since the publication of that letter, a great number have deserted their banners and turned traitor; very few comparatively have remained true to their oath of fidelity."

There are some terrible facts hidden from the people. "It is known that when Meade, a Roman Catholic, was to order the pursuit of Lee, after the battle of Gettysburg, a stranger came in haste to head-quarters, and that stranger, said Mr. Lincoln, was a distinguished Jesuit. After ten minutes' conversation with him, Meade made such arrangements for the pursuit of the enemy that he escaped almost untouched, with the loss of only two guns." (p. 702.)

"This letter of the Pope has changed the nature of the war. Before they read it, Roman Catholics could see that I was fighting against the Southern Confederacy, with Jefferson Davis at its head. But now they must believe that it is against Christ and his holy Vicar the Pope that I am raising my sacreligious hands. We have daily proof that their indignation, their hatred, their malice against me, are a hundredfold intensified. New projects of assassination are detected almost every day, accompanied with such savage circumstances that they bring to my memory the massacre of St. Bartholomew, and the gun-powder plot. We find on investigation, *that they come from the same masters in the art of murder, the Jesuits.*"

Then Mr. Lincoln declared that the New York riots were a Popish plot, and that

ARCHBISHOP HUGHES

102

was their instigator. When told by the President that he would be held responsible if they were not stopped, Archbishop Hughes faced the rioters, addressed them as friends, and invited them to go back home peacefully, and all was ended, after the most fiendish manifestations of hate, seen in the burning of the Colored Orphan Asylum and the trampling out of the lives of helpless children in their mad fury. We will not recount the bloody deed, though in the terrible treatment of John A. Kennedy and the murder of Col. O'Brien and his mutilation, we are reminded of the horrid barbarities inflicted upon Coligny in Paris, which shows that the spirit of Popery is unchanged.

THE TREACHERY OF ARCHBISHOP HUGHES

furnishes a terrible count in this indictment against Rome.

"I have," said Abraham Lincoln, "the proof that Archbishop Hughes, whom I had sent to Rome that he might induce the Pope to urge the Roman Catholics of the North at least to be true to their oaths of allegiance, and whom I thanked publicly when under the impression that he had acted honestly, according to the promise he had given me, is the very man who advised the Pope to recognize the legitimacy of the Southern Confederacy, and put the weight of his Tiara in the balance against us and in favor of our enemies. Such is the perfidy of Jesuits" (p. 704).

Two cankers are biting the very entrails of the United States,— the Romish and the Mormon priests. Both are aiming at the destruction of our schools, to raise themselves upon their ruins. Both shelter themselves under our grand and holy principles of liberty of conscience, to destroy that very liberty of conscience. The more dangerous of the two is the Jesuit priest, for he knows better how to conceal his hatred, under the mask of friendship and public good. He is better trained to commit the most cruel and diabolical deeds for the glory of God.

Abraham Lincoln had learned much, and unlearned much more. He declared himself to be

NOT IN FAVOR OF UNLIMITED TOLERATION

of Roman Catholics. "Once I was; now, it seems to me, that, sooner or later, the people will be forced to put a restriction to that clause of unlimited toleration toward Papists." "I am for liberty of conscience in its truest, noblest, broadest, highest sense. But I cannot give liberty of conscience to the Pope and his followers the Papists, so long as they tell me, through their councils, theologians, and canon laws, that their conscience orders them to burn my wife, strangle my children, and cut my throat when they find an opportunity" (p. 705).

"This does not seem to be understood by the people," continued Mr. Lincoln. "Sooner or later, the light of common sense will make it clear to everyone, that no liberty of conscience can be granted to men, who are sworn to obey a Pope who pretends to have the right to put to death those who differ from him in religion" (p. 706).

OUGHT ROMANISTS TO BE ALLOWED TO VOTE?

is beginning to be discussed. Father Hecker says: "The Roman Catholic is to wield his vote for the purpose of securing Catholic ascendency in this country." They vote as servants of the Pope, not as patriots.

It was stated by Pius IX: "The Catholic religion, with all its votes, ought to be exclusively dominant in such sort that every other worship be banished and interdicted."

We are putting into hands those potential ballots which will be, and are being, used against liberty. A theocracy controls them against which there is no protection. Emile DeLaveleye, the celebrated Belgian Liberal, has shown that an extended suffrage gives unlimited power to Rome in all those countries where her religion is the religion of the large mass of the people, and Gambetta's last letter contained this: "Do not adopt universal suffrage in your country; it will put you under the yoke of the clergy."

SAID ABRAHAM LINCOLN:

"From the beginning of the war, there has been, not a secret, but a public alliance between the Pope of Rome and Jeff. Davis, and that alliance has followed the common laws of the world's affairs. The greater has led the smaller; the stronger has guided the weaker. The Pope and his Jesuits have advised and directed Jeff. Davis on the land, from the first shot at Fort Sumter, by the rabid Roman Catholic Beauregard. They were helping him on the sea, by guiding and supporting the other rabid Roman Catholic, Pirate Semmes."

THE THOUGHT OF ASSASSINATION

was ever present. Warnings came to him from friends in America, and beyond the Sea. Secretary Stanton placed guards about him, at the Soldier's Home and at the White House. The President did not believe that these could secure him from harm. He lived with Christ and for men, and went on. Opening his Bible to Deut. 3: 22-28, the words made a profound impression upon his mind: "Ye shall not fear them; for the Lord your God shall fight for you." Then came the assurance that he was not to pass into the Canaan of peace. "Get thee up unto the top of Pisgah; look abroad; see the land and rest: for thou shalt not go over this Jordan."

His drawing near to God did him good. It is what we are, not what we profess, that tells the story. As Abraham Lincoln drew near to God, the people drew near to him. No longer was he called the horrid names which once characterized the opposition press. The God in him was conquering the devil about him. Each morning he gave a certain hour to reading the Scriptures and prayer, and came forth from his room ready for duty, with that light shining in his face which glorified Moses as he came down from the mount. This, while it made him friends with the soldiers and the people, maddened the Romanists.

In the light of what was to come so soon, we delight to go back and read statements like the following:

"When little Willie Lincoln died, the mind of the bereaved father was deeply affected by the thoughts of death. It was during the battle of Gettysburg that he shut himself up with God, and then such a sense of the presence of God and of his own unworthiness came to him and took possession of his soul, as to overwhelm him. From that day he dated his entrance into a new life. A Christian friend delighted to relate how, in the carriage, Mr. Lincoln begged the visitor to describe as clearly as possible what was the peculiar evidence which one might rely upon as assurance that he had become a Christian."

The simple story, as furnished by John, was repeated. It was explained, that when a poor sinner, conscious that he could not save himself, looked to Jesus Christ, saw in his death a full atonement for the sinner's sin, and believed that Christ's death was accepted as a substitute for the sinner's death, he felt himself to have been delivered from the Divine wrath, and to be at peace with God through our Lord Jesus Christ." The President, in a tone of satisfaction, said: "That is just the way I feel." All this paved the way for what was to come. The war was over, The soldiers of the Confederacy were going to rebuild their homes and to re-cultivate their fields, with blessings instead of cursings following them. Soup-houses had been placed for the starving at the base of flag-staffs, where the stars and bars had usurped the place belonging to the flag which is the ensign of hope for all lands and climes.

Friday, the 14th of April, 1865, had come. It was a day memorable in many ways. On this day, Beauregard had fired on Sumter. On this day, General Anderson, amid the thunder of cannon and the cheers of loyal hearts, had again raised the flag over the ruins of Sumter.

HIS LAST DAY ON EARTH

is noteworthy. He had written to a friend that he was going to use precaution. He had said: "The Jesuits are so expert in their deeds of blood, that Henry IV. said it was impossible to escape them, and he became their victim, though he did all he could to protect himself. My escape from their hands, since the letter of the Pope to Jeff. Davis has sharpened a million of daggers, is more than a miracle."

He breakfasts with his son, Captain Robert S. Lincoln, who was on General Grant's staff, having just returned from the capitulation of Lee, and the President passed a happy hour listening to all the details. At eleven o'clock he attended his last cabinet-meeting. When it was adjourned, Secretary Stanton said he felt that the Government was stronger than at any previous period since the Rebellion commenced; and the President is said, in his characteristic way, to have told them that some important news would soon come, as he had a dream of a ship sailing very rapidly, and had invariably had that same dream before great events in the war,—Bull Run, Antietam, Gettysburg.

WOLVES GO IN PACKS, AS DO SINS.

The invitation for President and Mrs. Lincoln, General and Mrs. Grant, Speaker Colfax and wife, to attend the theatre, is now known to have been a part of the plot. Lincoln, not because he loved the theatre or cared for the play, but to please the people and obtain needed rest, yielded to the persuasion of his wife, and to the sentiment which rules very largely the crowned heads of Europe,—when the king goes to his box in the theatre that the people might see him and that he might see the people. General Grant did not go, nor did Mr. Colfax, and other invited guests. Lincoln was disappointed; rode around with his wife and invited Colonel Rathbun and his wife to seats with them: they accepted the invitation and saw the horrid deed performed.

The box of the theatre was made ready for his assassination. John Wilkes Booth, an illegitimate son of his father, had been boasting for days in drunken moods of what he was to do. He had united with the Roman Catholic Church, though he was drinking to excess and plotting the murder of America's noblest citizen, with Roman Catholic priests, who instructed him and inducted him into the Church, and promised him protection and support in his nefarious crime.

In the book of testimonies given in the prosecution of the assassins of Lincoln, published by Ben Pitman, and in the two volumes of the trial of John Surratt, 1867, we have the legal and irrefutable proof that Rome directed the movements of Booth; that the plot was matured in the house of Mary Surratt, 561 H Street, Washington, D. C.; that Father Lehiman, a priest, made her house his home; that Father Wiget and other priests were constantly going in and out: and that all the details of the conspiracy were planned there and provided for. Booth was made to feel that he was the instrument of God in ridding the world of Lincoln. The day before his death, he wrote: "I can never repent, though I hated to kill. Our country owed all her troubles to him, Lincoln, and God simply made me the instrument of his punishment." So thought Ravillac, the assassin of Henry IV. Both were trained to believe that there was no sin in killing the enemy of the holy church and of the infallible Pope.

Let us draw aside the curtain:

PROOFS THAT ROMANISM WAS THE ASSASSIN OF ABRAHAM LINCOLN.

The evening came. The President is sitting in his box in the theatre. He is resting in a rocking chair. A man enters the door of the lobby leading to the box. He closes the door behind him. He draws a pistol, and shoots the President in the back of his head. The shriek of Mrs. Lincoln pierces the ears of all. Booth leaps upon the stage, brandishing a dagger, and flies, saying as he does, *"Sic semper tyrannis."* His horse at the door is held by a Roman Catholic. He leaps upon, it and rides away.

Proof that Rome directed the arm of J. Wilkes Booth is seen:

First.—In the fact that the house of Mrs. Surratt, a Roman Catholic, where the plot was laid, swarmed with priests.

Second.—The Mr. Lloyd, who kept the carbine which Booth wanted for protection, was a Roman Catholic.

Third.—Dr. Mudd, who set the leg of Booth, was a Roman Catholic.

Fourth.—Garrett, in whose barn Booth took refuge and where he was shot, was a Roman Catholic.

Fifth.—All the conspirators, says General Baker, the great detective, were attending Roman Catholic services, or were educated as Roman Catholics.

Sixth.—Priests sheltered and spirited away John Surratt, and Pope Pius IX. gave him a place among his guards,

Seventh.—The plot was known as far away as St. Joseph, Minn., 40 miles from a railroad, and more than 80 miles from a telegraph. Rev. F.

A. Conwell, late chaplain of a Minnesota regiment, was told at that place at six P.M. on April 14th, the night of the assassination, by the purveyor of the monastery filled with priests, that President Lincoln and Secretary Seward had been killed, four hours before the deed was attempted. How was it known? There is but one answer. The conspiracy which cost Abraham Lincoln his life was resolved upon by the priests of Washington and communicated to priests in far-away St. Joseph. Charles Boucher, a priest in Canada, swears that John Surratt was sent to him by Father Lefierre, the canon of the bishop of Montreal. For months he concealed him, and then shipped him to Rome. Why? Because it was in the bond. They promised the murderers protection on earth, so far as they could give it to them, and a crown in heaven if they died in the attempt.

Eighth.—The rejoicing of Romanists at the outset, and until they saw their peril. Mrs. Surratt, the day after the murder, said, without being rebuked, in the presence of several witnesses: "The death of Abraham Lincoln is no more than the death of any nigger in the army."

WHY WAS NOT MORE MADE OF IT?

Why is not more made of it? Cowardice explains it all. Fear was on every side. The leaders declared, We are just through with one war; if we make an attack on the Roman Catholic church and hang a few of their priests, who could be proven guilty of participating in the plot, a religious war would be the result. Nothing would have been easier than to have proven the criminality of the priests; but this was carefully avoided, from the beginning to the end of the trial. When their eyes were opened to their peril, the fear of the priests was pitiable. They say that their damning deed had frozen the milk in the breasts of millions. Jesuitism, with the tread of a panther and the cunning of a sleuthhound, shrank away, and hid from sight for the time. Alas! politicians seemed smitten with the same dread. Father Chiniquy declared that, when, not long after the execution of the murderers, he went incognito to Washington, to begin his investigations about the true and real authors of the deed, he was not a little surprised to see that not a single one of the men connected with the Government to whom he addressed himself would consent to have any talk with him on that matter, except after he had given his word of honor that he would never mention their names in connection with the result of the investigation. He says: "I saw with profound distress that the influence of Rome was almost supreme in Washington. I could not find a single statesman who would dare face the nefarious influence, and fight it down." This was the policy of Lincoln. On this rock his bark struck, and went down.

The Romanism that assassinated President Lincoln is in our midst, unchanged in spirit and in purpose. Upon the American people devolve fearful respon sibilities,

THINGS THAT CAN BE DONE.

First.—" We can tell the truth about Romanism."

Second.—" We can tell the truth to Romanists." *Third.*— " We can hold America for Americans." Had Abraham Lincoln voiced the utterance, it would have made him the evangel that would have carried hope to the millions of earth. The work he left undone we must undertake, and then shall Romanism find here a grave, into which the roots of liberty shall go and find nutriment, while above shall tower the hardy trunk, from whose wide branches shall hang fruits which, gathered by God's best children, shall fill the garners of hope, and make this Immanuel's Land.

10

Fifteen Thousand Slaves to Rome In Washington; or, Americans Under the Surveillance of Rome

IT WILL SURPRISE THE PEOPLE of the great free republic of the United States to learn that

FIFTEEN THOUSAND DEPARTMENT CLERKS

are under the surveillance of Rome. This seems like a strange statement. The many will say it cannot be true. The fact remains. Romanism is the dominant power in the Capital of the United States. The war which Rome helped to bring on, and which she hindered as best she could when she saw it was to eventuate in liberty, resulted in her advantage rather than to her detriment. The reason for it is difficult to explain. Had Abraham Lincoln told the truth about Romanism to the people, the curse would have been wiped out. The reason he did not, and gave for not doing it, influences thousands at the present time, viz.: *fear of a religious war.*

It seems inexplicable that the power which assassinated Abraham Lincoln should have been fostered and aided by the people who slew slavery and who recognized the fact that Romanism was its chief ally. Who can think of Thaddeus Stevens patting this monster that slew the great Emancipator, without a shudder of horror, mingled with a feeling of incredulity. A strange fear of Rome came upon the politicians of all parties after the civil war was over. Proofs abounded of the disloyalty of this life-long foe of liberty. They were unheeded. They remain unheeded. From dozens of letters, and from unnumbered clerks in the departments, information is furnished that, after the 1st and 15th of every month, nuns have the free run of the departments, and can ask every clerk and every head of a department for money to help on the Church of Rome. Some of these letters are sad beyond expression. The wife of a Union soldier writes: "I am in Department. There are nine Irish toone American. The persecution to which I am subjected, in hopes of driving me out, is difficult to describe and hard to bear. They preach their religion and their politics. If a word is said against it, the air is made blue with profanity, and such words as, 'Get out, you heretic; we'll make it hot for you,' are heard on every hand."

ROME HAS THE ENTRÉE

to any of the Departments, and can do what she desires. Any one without the black robe and bonnet would be thrust out by the door-keepers. These are admitted by special order. *Must this be borne? Is not this an outrage to Christian employees in a free Government?* Drop the word "Christian." Is it not an outrage on American citizenship? Has Rome any claim upon these clerks in the service of the Government? Suppose Baptists or Presbyterians should ask the privilege of going through the departments to solicit funds for church purposes, would the request be granted? Most assuredly not.

We have said the clerks were under the surveillance of Rome. Suppose they do not like it? What can they do about it? Seven men, members of the Grand Army of the Republic, some from Northern states, some from Southern, told how they were not only asked by these nuns to give twice a month, but that they were afraid not to give. They related how the heads of the departments are very largely either Roman Catholics, or afraid to antagonize them, and because one of their number expressed his mind in regard to the outrage of having these black-robed minions of Rome tramping through the departments and asking American citizens to contribute to the support of *"The Harlot of the Tiber"* his name was handed in as a man who had insulted a saintly nun, and at the close of the month his dismissal came, and no reasons given. They who refuse to give are reported, and when vacancies are required, their names are ready for use. The result need not be described. Fear of losing their places is everywhere apparent. It affects society, muzzles the press, and chains the pulpit.

If there is one doctrine distinctively American, it is that *there must be a separation between church and State.* If there is one doctrine distinctively democratic, it is that the State must support the representatives of the Church of Rome.

TALK ABOUT HOME RULE

for Ireland, we need it in Washington. The Capital, the Departments, the President's House, the Post Office, the Foreign, and now the Interior Department, are under the domination of Roman Catholics, the instigators of the Civil War and the assassins of Abraham Lincoln, the life-long foe of liberty here, and throughout the world.

THE TROUBLE IN WASHINGTON

lies in the fact, that the men in office live, when at home, in different places, which are also under the dominance of Rome.

Several members of Congress related that it is the custom of the nuns to visit every member of Congress soon after he arrives: they ask for a contribution. If they give, well. If not, it is reported.

HOW THE NUNS WERE DRIVEN OUT.

A Northern lady, a good Baptist, whose husband is independent of public patronage, rented rooms to a member of Congress. Hardly had he got his trunk unstrapped, before two nuns came. The girl let them in. They were asked to call again after the gentleman got settled. They were no sooner out, than the lady of the house said: "If those women come again, seat them in the hall, and don't let them in until I see them." The next day they were seated in the hall, and she came down. The lady is utterly fearless, and has no respect for, nor fear of black-robed Sisters of Charity.

"What do you want?"

"To see the Member of Congress"

"What for?"

"To see him."

"He has a wife, and don't need the attentions of other women."

"We wish to see him for the church."

"He is not a Roman Catholic, and has a better church, which he helps support."

Then the old nun claimed she wished to go into a private room to fix her shoe. "Fix it here: you are not afraid of me, are you?"

Then she spoke up, and asked: "Do you refuse to let me see a Member of Congress in this house?"

"*I do.*"

"Then we will take the number of this house, and it may be to your injury."

"All right; take it, and advertise it, if you choose; my house cannot be made a run-way for Romish hirelings."

It is a simple fact, that the house is always full of occupants, and is felt to be a retreat from the incursions of Romanists.

Is there any good reasons why the Roman Catholic church should become a universal beggar, and yet house the Pope in the largest palace in the world, and feed her cardinals, bishops, lady-superiors, priests and nuns on the fat of the land?

Was there ever a set of dupes like Romanists, who, as a rule, live in squalor, while the money drawn from the poor is placed on the largest structures of the land.

ROME IS NOT POOR.

More wealth is under her control than is possessed by the representative of any nation, sect, or faith. Her wealth is a secret. Out of Peter's Pence comes a great patrimony. Rome claims to be beneficent, and so becomes the recipient of bounty from the State, as well as from individuals. No sect is less so. No people give so little to any object outside of their own communion.

fifteen hundred feet in length, eight hundred in breadth, with twenty courts, miles of galleries filled with pictures and statuary, two hundred stair-cases, eleven hundred rooms, the construction of which has cost more than one hundred millions of dollars, and yet he is the pensioner of the whole world!

As a rule, the people who belong to the Church of Rome are poor. In Roman Catholic countries where Romanism rules supreme, they are very poor. In Ireland, in the Roman Catholic districts, the men and women sleep in ditches and herd with pigs. It is surprising that, in New York, Romanists, living in tenement houses, in garrets and cellars, are content to abide in squalor, while the archbishop, whose iron hand was laid on every free impulse, and all who sympathized with it, lives in a palace, and is fed on food that befits the table of a king. The Pope has for his own use four Palatine cardinals, three prelates, and a master, ten prelates of the private chamber, amongst whom are cupbearers and keepers of the wardrobe, two hundred and fifteen domestic prelates, and more than four hundred women. Then follows two hundred and forty-nine supernumerary prelates of the private chamber, four private chamberlains of the sword and cloak, Roman patricians, a quarter-master, major, a correspondent-general of the post, one hundred and thirty fresh private chamberlains of the sword and cloak. Next come two hundred and sixty-five honorary monsignori, extra urbem, six honorary chamberlains of the sword and cloak, then eight private chaplains; then two private monsignori of the tonsure,—or, *barbers in short,* but monsignori just the same; then eighteen supernumeraries. In all, one thousand and twenty-five persons; besides the Palatine administration and the tribunal of the major-domo,—the Swiss guards—the gens d'arms, and a legion of servants. Does it not need a brazen effrontery, which is astonishing, to send priests and nuns all over the world to extract the pence from the pockets of the poor, to keep in luxury this army of men, for the most part privates, who earn not a dollar, and are utterly worthless as aids to humanity? If it be difficult for a rich man to enter into the kingdom of heaven, how shall he who inherits the Vatican enter there, who has treasures of all sorts, many precious gems, countless works of art, vessels of silver and gold, and more than a thousand servants? On his head is not one crown, but three. He is borne on the shoulders of men. He compels his votaries to kiss his toe, and enjoys an income of millions.

In the United States, the attempt is being made to rival Europe. The Cardinal's palace in New York, built of marble, filled with choice works of art, cost an immense sum. The dwellings of bishops and priests are planned on a magnificent scale. The gate into Rome is not strait, and the way is not narrow. They can carry with them bad politics, bad principles, bad practices and bad lives, and yet if they will give their consciences to the priests, and believe what they are taught concerning penance, absolution, forms and ceremonies, the conditions of becoming a Roman Catholic are met. A change of heart is not in the programme. A blameless, pure life is not in the bond. It is not strange that error thrives beneath the shadow of Romanism. Rum selling is not a sin, and if rum-drinking were even a disgrace, few are the priests who would be respectable. Mormonism fattens on polygamy, and Mohammedanism, that painted a heaven in which lust should have full play, and the bestial nature supremacy, won a large following, and holds it, because the carnal heart can there find full play for passion and desire. Romanism is a match for either Mormonism or Mohammedanism. The priests practice polygamy under another name, and find in the church a *carte blanche* for the promptings of the natural heart.

ROMANISM IS A DECEPTION AND A FRAUD.

A deception, because it claims to have been built on St. Peter in Rome; when there is not a scintilla of evidence that Peter ever saw Rome. He was the apostle of the circumcision. He went to Babylon, and from there wrote his epistles. Paul went to Rome, and called the names of the prominent ones he met; but never mentioned Peter, who lived and died in the East. But Romanism without Peter in Rome is a failure; and so the lie, that he came to Rome, lived there twenty-five years, was in the Marmantine Prison over which St. Peter's towers, and died crucified head downwards, in the place upon which the Vatican stands, where the Pope lives, all this is unblushingly lifted into prominence as if it were a truth, when all history knows it to be false.

Romanism is a fraud because it pretends to have power which does not belong to it. Tradition usurps the place of Scripture, it subordinates the inward and spiritual to the outward and visible; it obscures and stifles the life of faith and love, by its absorbing attention to the things of sight and show; instead of relying on Jesus, who is the Christ, and was offered once for all, it makes a new Jesus and a new atonement at every Mass; instead of having one mediator between God and man (1 Timothy, ii. 5), it makes the mother of Jesus both a mediator and a God, and treats, likewise, its thousands of other canonized (real or unreal) saints as mediators, to be prayed to and honored for their superhuman merit and power. By its connected doctrines of confession and penance, and absolution and indulgence, it places the consciences, persons, and property of many women and children in the power of the priest; it speaks lies in hypocrisy, sears the conscience as with a hot iron; it changes the truth of God into a lie, and worships and serves the creature more than the Creator; it turns the consolations and comforts of religion, the means of grace, and the hope of glory, into so much merchandise, to be disposed of according to the vender, and the ability or necessity of the purchaser; in fine, it sets forth another gospel than the free gospel of Christ, another standard than the perfect law of God, other ordinances and other conditions of salvation than those which the Lord Jesus has established. It has fellowship with darkness rather than light, and is in affinity with Satan and his angels, rather than with Jehovah. And yet, bad as it is in character and in practice, the Republic of the United States gives to this assassin of President Lincoln, to this enemy of all righteousness, to this instigator of the civil war, rights denied to the representatives of Jesus Christ's Gospel, and compels fifteen thousand employees of the Government to give to its support, or to have their places endangered, and their living confiscated!

Romanism is a fraud, because it claims to be in line with apostolic succession, when there have been at least thirty schisms in the church.

Two popes have claimed St. Peter's chair at one and the same time, and fought and led armies to maintain the supremacy. In 1414, the Council of Constance cashiered three popes, John XXIII., Gregory XIII. and Benedict XIII. as deserving the deepest execration, and as guilty of most horrible crimes.

Popes have been guilty of the most horrible practices. What matters it though Pope Joan was taken with the pains of childbirth on a public parade, though mistresses and harlots had control of the Chair, Rome as unblushingly holds out her pauper hand and cries *Give!* as if she had a good history, and was backed by a decent life! Romanism is indifferent to Scripture and public opinion.

Romanists want a Peter for Rome, and they get him. In spite of Scripture, they will hold on to him; and for all Scripture can do, Peter may yet become a second Romulus, suckled by a wolf, and the founder of the Eternal City. It would be as true as much of the history they are making for the youth of America.

Is it not enough to tolerate Romanism? Shall the free people of America be compelled to give to its support? Shall this church be permitted to dominate the State? This is being done in many portions of the Republic. Shall a halt be called?

This question must be answered. Romanism is for the first time uncovering its intent in America, and revealing the fact that the spirit of hellish hate which dominated the organism in Spain, and also in Italy, characterizes it in the Republic, where, it was said, free institutions were to change its purpose and modify its nature. A good time to answer the question has come. Freemen are at last beginning to understand that freedom is in peril. Romanists who hope for better things are tiring of the old despotism, and are beginning to seek for the new life.

11

The Lap of Rome

IN A CITY CURSED WITH malaria is a cesspool, so large that it spreads contagion through many cellars, up into offices, into stores, and infects the town. In winter, they do not clean it out, because of the cold. In summer, they have another excuse. It is covered with boards. Ever and anon one rots. A horse breaks through and is ruined. A man falls in and dies. Then comes a spasm of indignation, and many declare the cesspool must go; but it stays; it is working mischief.

Romanism is much like it. It poisons the air and affects the health, wherever its virus is inhaled. It is bad, and bad continually. Few care to touch it, or describe it. The cesspool is covered over. It ought to be cleaned out, but it is not. There are reasons why the many fail to attack the error or fight the sin. It controls votes—how many, few know. The leaders of the Romish cohort are astute, far-seeing and brave. They work together, strike an organized blow, are conscienceless, and so are never hindered by principle or restrained by honor, Tightness or righteousness. They are a bandit against virtue, education and progress. They are not ashamed of it. They will shut the best histories out of the school. There is a spasm. Meetings are held; Rome is attacked, and Rome is silent; *but the books stay out,* and Protestant teachers turn Catholics for place and pelf, and Rome laughs and moves on, securing the acquiescence, if not the favor, of politicians. So in regard to morality. A man breaks through into the cesspool. He is covered with filth. Romanism is revealed, and the people declare now it must go; but a new board is laid over the hole; lime is thrown in; the stench is killed for the moment, and Rome increases in power. Rome stands by Rome—as true men would do well to stand by true men, but as true men seldom do,— while the emergency is on, and help is needed.

"Why Priests Should Wed," was written to save women and girls threatened by the filth of the Confessional. Much that is vile, and too filthy to be read with pleasure or profit to the individual perusing it, has been omitted. For this, the author has been blamed by good men and women. "We do not know about it," they say. "You say, there is a cesspool. You say it is beyond human belief for vileness. We do not have more than the words of men like you. The offensive matter is locked up in Latin. It is beyond our reach. This thing of Romanism concerns Americans. Romanism is doing all in its power to capture the United States. It will succeed, unless the truth be told concerning it." Such is the view of good Christian men.

Romanism is bringing forth as bad fruit in Washington as elsewhere. Assaults are made on virtue. Nunneries are used as assignation houses there as elsewhere, because Romanists live there as elsewhere. This ought to be brought to the attention of the people, if they are to be delivered. It is fashionable to speak of Romanism as a part of the Christian world. Encyclopedias do it; so do ministers of Evangelical denominations. It is a shame that this is true, yet true it is. Romanism is the "mystery of iniquity." It is a horrible stench in the nostrils of humanity, borne because of the lack of power to remove it. Hated of God, it is yet to be hated of man.

But, in the meantime, the people have a battle to wage with error, and a duty to discharge. Romanism must be exposed. Uncover the cesspool, and it shall bring upon itself destruction.

In "Why Priests Should Wed," Dens and Liguori were quoted, and all that could be decently written was put into type, and a challenge was sent forth asking Romanists to deny it, if they could; or for Congress to appoint a Commission to investigate the charges brought against the priesthood of the Roman Catholic church because of the practice of Auricular Confession, and to demand persons and papers competent, in evidence, to declare whether such confessional is calculated to pollute the minds of the people, and undermine the foundation of our Republican institutions. Thousands and tens of thousands of these petitions were signed and sent to and read in the Senate and House of Representatives, and nothing has been done about it.

In the meantime, the author congratulates himself as having "built better than he knew," because Romanists know what is left out in the blank spaces as Protestants do not, and the effect of the book has been helpful to Romanists, great numbers of whom, because of its appalling revelations, have abandoned Rome forever. It has been charged that, in "Why Priests Should Wed," the quotations are largely from Dens and Liguori, and not from theologians of the Roman Catholic Church in America. This was because Dens' theology has been endorsed by the prelates in Ireland as the *best book on the subject* that *could be* published, as late as Sept. 15th, 1808, and by the Archbishop of St. Louis, Mo., in Feb. 1850, by Bishop Kenrick of Philadelphia, in 1861. A thousand dollars reward was offered in 1873 to any accredited Roman priest or bishop who will disprove the horrible disclosure contained in a book translating the Latin into English and German, from the Secret Theology of Peter Dens and Francis P. Kenrick, published in Chicago, 111. No reply has been made, because a refutation is impossible.

The truth is not hidden; but it is not scattered. Show what Romanists are, what they teach, and how they live, and decent people will cut loose from it; and the President, unless he be lost to all self-esteem and sense of decency, and the respect of mankind, would as soon walk the streets with a painted representative of the house which is "the way to hell, going down to the chambers of death," as to lock arms with the Red-Robed Cardinal, the representative of the Harlot of the Tiber.

It is not necessary to confine attention to the works of Dens and Liguori. John Hughes, archbishop of New York, and Francis Patrick Kenrick, archbishop of Philadelphia, have sanctioned all the vileness of the past, and sent forth contributions as vile as any that preceded. These are accessible. In the book, "Theology in Use in the Theological Seminary and Sacred Theology for Students," by Francis Patrick Kenrick, are descriptions of "adulterers with the mouth" (p. 130), of the manner in which the marriage bed is to be used and is defiled (1. vi., n. 917), and suggestions concerning intercourse too filthy to be written; of the sin of evading offspring, and the means employed to produce the result; of the guilt of Sodomy, and how the sin is committed between husband and wife (l.vi., n. 916) ; of the sin of rendering one's-self impotent, and much more in the same strain.

PARISH PRIESTS AND OTHER CONFESSORS PROVIDED FOR.

Because this is frequently denied, we quote in full;

"VIII. *Of Luxury.* If, however, it should be foreseen that pollution will ensue from some cause that is necessary, or useful, or advantageous to somebody, although the mind is averse to it, there is no sin, so long as there is no danger in consenting to it. Hence, even though involuntary pollution should be foreseen, it is proper for,

"1. Parish Priests, and also other confessors, to hear the confessions of women, to read treatises on obscene subjects, to touch the parts of a sick woman, to accost, kiss or embrace women according to the custom of the country, to wait on them in bathing, and other things of a similar character.

"2. It is lawful for any one who suffers great itching in the privates, to relieve it by touching, although pollution may follow.

"3. So also it is useful to ride on horseback for a person, even though pollution should be foreseen," and much more of the same character.

"4. It is lawful to lie in any position to rest more conveniently.

"5. To take warm food or drinks, in moderation, and to lead in decent dances."*

Into this lap of Rome, look. The Parish Priest is given absolute control of the bodies of the women of the Roman Catholic church, and of all others he may capture. Liguori grants a priest two women a month. Kenrick permits a lascivious scoundrel to gratify his lustful inclinations. When wife or daughter is the victim, does not the permission given in the theology place the entire church under

---

* Francis Patrick Kenrick's Theology, vol. 3, p. 172.

suspicion? *Somebody's* daughter, *somebody's* wife shut up with the priest in the Confessional, or in his home, is his victim.

Let us turn now to the "Garden of the Soul," a prayer-book commonly used in the Roman Catholic churches, and for sale at all Roman Catholic bookstores, and commended by Archbishop Hughes, and on pages 213 and 214 are these questions, to be asked by a Roman Catholic priest of any female, from seven up to seventy.

"Have you been guilty of fornication, or adultery, or incest, or any sin against nature, either with a person of the same sex, or with any other creature? How often? Or have you designed or attempted any such sin, or sought to induce others to it? How often?

"Have you been guilty of pollution, or immodest touches of yourself? How often?

"Have you touched others, or permitted yourself to be touched by others immodestly? or given and taken wanton kisses, or embraces, or any such liberties? How often?

"Have you looked at immodest objects, with pleasure or danger? read immodest books, or songs, to yourself, or others? kept indecent pictures? willingly given car to, and taken pleasure in hearing loose discourses? or sought to see or hear anything that was immodest? How often?

"Have you exposed yourself to wanton company? or played at any indecent play? or frequented masquerades, balls, comedies, with danger to your chastity? How often?

"Have you been guilty of any immodest discourse, wanton stares, jests, or songs, or words of double meaning? and how often? and before how many? and were the persons to whom you spoke or sung married or single? For all this you are obliged to confess, by reason of the evil thoughts these things are apt to create in the hearers.

"Have you abused the marriage-bed by any action contrary to the order of nature? or by any pollutions? or been guilty of any irregularity, in order to hinder your having children? How often? (Ways to ascertain all this are pointed out by Bishop F. P. Kenrick, in the theology which every priest must study). Have you, without just cause, refused the marriage debt? and what sin followed from it? How often?

"Have you debauched any person that was innocent before? Have you forced any person, or deluded any one by deceitful promises, etc.? or designed, or desired to do so? How often?

"Have you taught any one evil that he knew not of before? or carried any one to lewd houses?" etc. How often?"

"Have you willingly taken pleasure in unchaste thoughts or imaginations? or entertained unchaste desires? Were the objects of your desires maids, or married persons, or kinsfolks, or persons consecrated to God? How often?

"Have you taken pleasure in the irregular motions of the flesh? or not endeavored to resist them? How often?

"Have you entertained with pleasure the thoughts of saying or doing anything which it would be a sin to say or do? How often?

"Have you had the desire or design of committing any sin,—of what sin? How often?"

Can an unmarried priest ask these questions of the women of his flock, full of life, of blood, of impure thoughts, without finding out all he wants to know to ascertain where victims for his lust abide? These questions are asked in every town where is a Roman Catholic church, and lives growing out of them are lived; and this places the cesspool, full of concontagion, in juxtaposition with us all. Paul asked: "Shall I then take the members of Christ, and make them the members of a harlot? God forbid. What! know you not that he which is joined to a harlot, is one body?"* The fact is apparent, whoever tolerates Romanism tolerates harlotry of the worst and vilest descriptions.

TURN NOW TO DENS, WHO IS AUTHORITY.

---

* 1 Cor. 6: 15,16.

"A confessor has seduced his penitent to the commission of carnal sin, not in confession, nor by occasion of confession, but from some extraordinary occasion. Is he to be denounced?

"A. No. If he had tampered with her from his knowledge of confession, it would be a different thing, because, for instance, he knows that person, from her confession, to be given to such carnal sins."

Imagine a girl, fallen through the misconduct of a priest. She becomes alarmed. She goes to another confessor; tells her story. Confessors are advised not lightly to give credit to any woman whatsoever accusing their former confessor, but first to search diligently into the end and cause of the occasion, to examine their morals and conversation. *In other words, break down the witness.* "For which reason, observe, that whatever person, either by herself or by another, falsely accuses or denounces a priest as a seducer, incurs a case reserved for the supreme Pontiff." (Antoine, p. 428.) There is no protection for virtue in the Roman Catholic Church. The priest tells the woman she does not sin by yielding. He confesses to a priest and is absolved. All unite against virtue. Is not the window open? Cannot men see the character of Romanism to which the Republic and the United States surrenders?

WHAT WILL CITIZENS OF THE REPUBLIC DO ABOUT IT?

This is the question which must be answered by Christian men and women.

Nuns walk the streets of Washington in procession, with smiling faces, and defiant, don't-care look: sleek priests dwell in palatial residences, and have things their own way. Members of Congress surrender their wives and daughters to their care. Vast sums are given to propitiate the favor of Rome. The peril increases; not because Romanists outnumber Protestants, but because Protestants are silent who ought to speak.

THERE IS THE LAP OF ROME,

in Washington! The Nation's Capital has fallen into it, and ministers are as silent about it as if there were no peril. For shame! ! !

All this shows, as was said in "Why Priests Should Wed," that Francis Patrick Kenrick and John Hughes, who wrote, must have had an acquaintance and a practice in indulgence entirely opposed to the profession of celibacy or the existence of virtue. The book of Kenrick and the "Garden of the Soul" ought to be suppressed by legal enactment, and Auricular Confession should be banished from the Roman Catholic Church in America. Polygamy among Mormons is virtue personified, in comparison. Auricular confession is now the prolific source of gross licentiousness, and is destructive of virtue in the hearts of the priests who officiate in the Confessional. These infernal questions, framed by Bishops Kenrick and Hughes, propounded by bachelor priests to females of all ages, from seven years and upwards, and the obligation of the Confessional, binding them under pain of Eternal Damnation to eternal secrecy, is bringing forth a terrible harvest of lust and crime.

Rome does not preach, she plots. Rome cares not for public opinion or public remonstrances, so long as she can control votes, and get on increasing in wealth and power. In Eugene Sue's "Wandering Jew," Jesuits are uncovered in their hellish plottings and intrigues. The American of to-day ought to read that book of yesterday, for it reveals what practices, what machinations, what slavery, what abject ruin confronts the young men who shall give themselves to the control of the Jesuits in the American University now being built at Washington. One of the most beautiful characters in literature is *"Gabriel the priest."* An orphan, placed in the care of good and honest Catholics—if such there are—is surrendered by them to the Jesuits, because of facts which came to them concerning property on the way to a certain family, which the Jesuits determine to obtain and hold. As a result, for years, the plottings go on, that orphans may be robbed, and good and innocent people may be deprived of their rights.

Of the general course of education, it is not necessary to speak. It has been described a thousand times. It is the same at this time as in the days that are gone. But of the training much ought to be said. Gabriel enters the college. He says: "On the day of my joining it, the Superior said to me, in pointing out two of the pupils a little older than myself,' These are the companions with whom you are to associate: you will walk with them always, *but all three together*; the rules of the House forbidding any conversation between two persons alone."" The students from the Jesuit College in Washington go in threes, not in twos. Americans see it, and do not fight it.

TRAINED TO BE SPIES.

"'The same regulation enjoins, that you should listen attentively to what your companions may say, in order that you may report it to me, for those dear children may have, unknown to themselves, evil thoughts, or may contemplate the committing of a fault; but if you love your comrades, you must apprize me of their evil inclinations, in order that my paternal remonstrances may spare punishment, by preventing offence; for it is always better to prevent a fault than to punish it.'

"It happened sometime after, that I myself had been guilty of an infraction of the rules of the House; on which occasion the Superior said to me: 'My child! you have deserved a severe punishment, but you shall be pardoned, if you will promise to detect one of your companions in the same fault that you have committed.'" And all this is done in the name of all that is most holy.

Gabriel ashamed of such conduct, asked if it were wrong to be an informer. The answer: "A student has no right to discriminate between right and wrong, but only to obey; that to the confessor belonged the responsibility," uncovers the fetters that binds those under the control of Jesuits. His life was spent in an atmosphere of terror, of oppression, and suspicious watchings. Every effort is made to close the heart against all the gentle and tender emotions; to make of every young man a sneak, a hypocrite, a traitor.

Lying follows in the wake of such teaching. According to the Constitution of the Society of Jesus, this is trivial. Now let us see the outcome. The education in the college is finished. Into the seminary

Gabriel went, comparatively innocent. He was now to be prepared for the holy ministry. Let us see how the work goes on.

"'*You placed in my hands a book,*' he said, "'containing the questions that a confessor should put to young men, to young girls, to married women, when they presented themselves at that tribunal of penitance.'" "My God," exclaimed Gabriel, trembling, " I shall never forget that terrible moment. It was in the evening, I withdrew to my room, taking that book with me, composed, as you told me, by one of the fathers, and revised by a holy bishop." "It is impossible," said Eugene Sue, writing for the French, "to give even in Latin an idea of the infamous book."

Said Mr. Given, in his bold, excellent work, "*Of the Jesuit and the University:*" "I experience considerable embarrassment in commencing this chapter, as it has to treat of a book that it is impossible to translate, and difficult to cite from its text; because the Latin insults modesty by its plain speaking. I must, therefore, crave the indulgence of the reader, and will promise him in return to withhold as much obscenity as I can." Further on, in reference to the question imposed by the compendium, Mr. Given exclaims, with generous indignation: "What then must be the conversations that pass, in the retirement of the Confessional, between the priest and a married woman? I forbear to say more."

The author of the "Discoveries of the Bibliophilist," after having literally cited a great many passages from this horrible catechism, says: "My pen refuses to proceed further in this encyclopedia of every baseness, and I am sorry that it has gone so far; but I can only say, that though a mere copyist, I feel as much horror as if I had been touching poison. And yet, nevertheless, it is this horror that gives me courage. In the church of Jesus Christ, agreeably to the order established by the Divine will, that evil is good which leads one from error; and the more prompt the remedy the more it is efficacious. Morality can never be in danger so long as truth raises its voice and makes itself heard."

Gabriel describes the effect upon him as he read the book: "Full of respect, confidence and faith, I opened its pages. At first, I did not understand it; but at last I did. Struck with shame and horror, and overcome by astonishment, I had hardly strength to close, with trembling hand, this abominable textbook. I immediately came to you, my father, to ask pardon for having involuntarily cast my eyes on its pages, which, by mistake, I supposed you had put into my hands."

"'You may also remember,'" said the priest, "'that I quieted your scruples, explaining to you that it was necessary that a priest, who was destined to hear all things under the seal of confession, should know all, with the power of appreciating it; that the Society imposed the reading of the compendium as a text-book on you deacons, seminarists and priests, who might be called to the sacred duty of confession.'"

"'I believed you, my father; the habit of passive obedience was too strong upon me, discipline had so utterly deprived me of all self-examination, that spite of my horror, for which I then reproached myself as for a heavy fault, in remembering your words, I returned with the book into my room. I read it! Oh! my father, what a revelation was there of the excessive refinements of criminal luxury! Then in the vigor of youth, I had been alone upheld by my ignorance, and the assistance of God, against sensual struggles. Oh, that night, that night! in the midst of the deep silence of my solitude, trembling with fright and confusion, I spelt over that catechism of monstrous, unheard-of, unknown debaucheries; in proportion as its obscene pictures of frightful lust were presented to my imagination—till then chaste and pure,—you know, oh God! that it seemed as if my reason had become weakened; yes, and had entirely gone astray; for although I desired utterly to fly from this infernal book; yet, I know not by what awful, frightful attraction, by what devouring curiosity, I was still held breathless over its infamous pages. I felt as though I should have died from shame and confusion; and yet, in spite of myself, my cheeks were burning and a corrupting warmth circulated through my veins, and these terrible allusions assisted to complete my wanderings; it seemed as though lascivious phantoms were starting from its accursed pages, and I lost my recollection in seeking to avoid their burning embraces.'

"'The terms in which you speak of this book are highly blameable,' said the priest; 'you were the victim of your own excited imagination, and it is to that alone that you ought to ascribe those fatal impressions, instead of imputing them to a book, excellent and irreproachable for its purpose, and authorized by the church.'

"'Truly, my father,'" replied Gabriel, with the most profound bitterness, "'I have no right to complain that my mind, till that time innocent and pure, should henceforth be polluted with deformities that I should never even have dreamt of; for it is not likely that any who could have given themselves over to such horrors would have asked pardon from them of a priest.'

"'These are matters on which you are not competent to judge,' angrily replied the Father d' Aigrigny.

Then I will say no more on that subject,'" said Gabriel, as he proceeded.

"A long illness succeeded this awful night." After it, he went as a missionary to America. It is refreshing to read his description of his enjoyment of freedom:

"From my childhood, I had always either lived in a college or a seminary, in a state of oppression and continual dejection; and from being always accustomed to keep my eyes upon the ground, I had never known what it was to contemplate the heavens, or the splendid beauties of Nature. Oh, what profound, what religious happiness I enjoyed on first suddenly finding myself transported amongst the imposing grandeurs of the ocean, when, during the voyage, I contemplated myself between the sea and sky I Then it seemed as if I had quitted a place of thick and heavy darkness. For the first time for many years, I felt my heart freely beating in my bosom. For the first time, I felt that I was master of my own thoughts; and I then dared to examine my past life, as one who looks from a precipice into the deep and darkened valley beneath him. Then strange doubts came across my mind. I inquired of myself by what right, or to what end, I had been so long a time oppressed and borne down; deprived of the exercise of my free will, of my liberty, of my reason. Since God had endowed me with all these, then I reasoned, that perhaps the ends of that grand, beautiful and holy work to which I had dedicated myself, would one day be developed, and compensate me for my obedience and resignation.

On my arrival at Charleston, S. C., the Superior of the establishment in that town, to whom I had communicated my doubts as to the object of the Society, took upon himself to clear them up. With a fearful candor he unveiled their ends; not perhaps as understood by all the members of the Society, of whom a great many partook of my ignorance, but such as the principals of it had undeviatingly pursued from the foundation of the Order. I became terrified. I read the casuists. Oh, my father! what a new and frightful revelation for me, when at every page of these books, written by the fathers, I read *an excuse*—indeed a justification—*of robbery, calumny, violation, adultery, perjury, murder, regicide,* as follows:

"Violation.—He who, either by force, menace, fraud, or importunity, seduces a virgin, without promise of marriage, must indemnify the girl, or her relative.-, for the wrong that may result from it, by giving her *a* dowry, by which she may get a husband; or marrying her himself, if he cannot otherwise indemnify her. *If, however, the offense remains an absolute secret, the seducer is not bound to make any restitution."* This is Romanism.

"Adultery.—If any one has a guilty connection with a married woman, not because she is married, but because she is handsome— setting aside the circumstances of her being married—such connection, according to many authors, does not constitute the sin of adultery, but merely that of fornication."

After reading this, Gabriel said: "When I thought within myself, that as a priest of the God of charity, of justice, of pardon, I yet belonged to a society whose chiefs propounded such doctrines and boasted of them, I made an oath before God, to break forever the bonds by which I was attached to it."

Is it probable, is it possible, that Jesuitism has improved? Is such a school or university a desideratum in this land? Do we need to have American youth doomed to such a discipline? Father Chiniquy declares, that students in this land seek to escape this sea of nastiness. The effect of such teaching is horrible. It undermines and degrades manhood. It is time that this truth was brought home to the consciences of men. They

131

have got to be made to see that Romanism is not a religion, but a plot—an adjunct of hell; and that it has nothing whatever to do with heaven.

Now it is admitted, that the most revolting and degrading scene of the confessional is that of the prescribed treatment of females. On the mind of every Roman Catholic the conviction is fastened, that damnation is sure to come to those who go to confession and do not confess every sin they have committed. Further, that if a female appears modest, the confessor is instructed that her modesty must be overcome, or else he is authorized to deny her absolution.

"But," it has been well asked, "what modesty in a young lady, or any other person, is in danger of being offended, if the priest's conduct is directed by God's word? For then he would think of and practice naught but 'whatsoever things are true, whatsoever things are honest, whatsoever things are pure, whatsoever things are lovely, and whatsoever things are of good report.' It is, however, because of the opposite of those things, especially in things that *we pure,* that the modesty of the most hardened sinner must at times be shocked in the confessional; of course, we need not be surprised to learn that a young lady can be offended there. Indeed, in looking over a pamphlet, containing lengthy extracts from theological works used in seminaries, not in Ireland, but in the United States, that part of the confessional having reference particularly to females,—in single life, in the marriage state, and in widowhood,—it is impossible to conceive of anything more vile, more outrageously offensive and abominable, to any mind not steeped in the lowest depths of sensualized life." Ought not these facts to be placed within reach of the fathers and mothers whose children are exposed to such perils because the Roman Catholic Church is permitted unmolested to do its hellish work? Approach it and try to write the words, and the hand pauses, the heart sickens, and it seems impossible to proceed.

How husbands can allow their wives to go to confession, fathers their daughters, brothers their sisters; or how an intelligent and thoughtful people can look with favor upon the building up of an institution in which these debasing and polluting utterances are taught, passes comprehension.

The Rev. Pierce Connelly, a domestic chaplain to the Earl of Shrewsbury, in a letter published in the *London Times,* says: "I have had experience in the confessional, from princes downwards, and out of it, such as perhaps has fallen to the lot of no other living man; and my solemn conviction is, that a celibate priesthood, organized like that of Rome, is in irreconcilable hostility with all good human interests. I have seen clerical inviolability made to mean nothing less than license and impurity. I have read to the simple-minded Cardinal-Prefect of the Propaganda a narrative written to a pious lady friend, by a respected Roman priest, of such enormities of lust in his fellow priests around him, that the reading of them took away the breath; to be answered,— 'Caro Mio' —'T know it, I know it all, and more and worse than all; but nothing can be done!' I have known a priest practice Ligouri on his client simply as an amateur of wickedness, apparently without conscious malice, just as he would try poison upon dogs and cats; an Iago, without even an imaginary wrong from anybody,* and I have seen priests of mean abilities, of coarse natures, and gross breeding, practice upon pure and highly-gifted women of the upper ranks, married and unmarried, the teachings of their treacherous and impure casuistry, and with a success that seemed more than human. I have seen these priests impose their pretended divine authority, and sustain it by mock miracles, for ends that were simply devilish. I have had poured into my ears what can never be uttered, and what ought not to be believed, but was only too plainly true. And I have seen that all that is most deplorable *is not an accident, but a result, and an inevitable result, of the working practical system of the church of Rome, with all its stupendous machinery of mischief. And the system is irrevocable and irremediable.'*†

Yet this is not all. It is even not the worst. Man is what woman makes him, and the priest unmakes the woman and subverts the solid

---

* Letters of Marcus, p. 122.
† *Ibid,* p. 122

133

edifice by the ruin of the foundation. What shall be done about it? Shall the truth be scattered? The need of it is apparent in this and other lands.

The Chairman of the Chili Mission of the Presbyterian church, writes as follows:

"My Dear Brother: I have read your book 'Why Priests Should Wed,' and beg to say it is just what is needed. I wish you had the power of reading the secrets of the greatest secret society in the world— the Roman Catholic Church,—as these secrets are hidden to-day in the United States. I could give you some live facts of the present moment concerning the great Harlot as this immense institution has developed here.

"I will write my request, and then give you a fact or two illustrative of the BEAST you are trying to destroy: 1. Have you any objections to our translating and printing your book in Chili? 2. Would you object to its coming out in Spanish *in an unmutilated form?* and if so, *would you be willing to supply us the suppressed matter so that it could be restored in the translation?* Let me add now a fact or two that will illustrate, 1st: Your theme, 'Why Priests Should Wed;' and secondly, The benumbing influence of this horrid system, on not only the conscience, but also on the moral sense of the Romanist, and the manliness and womanliness of the members of this depraved society.

"The Sota-Cura, or Vice-Cura, in Parral, ruined, sometime ago, one of the teachers in the public school. The lady lives now in San Carlos, and the child is in Chilan, and the Cura still performs his functions.

"The Principal Cura of Parral says, that it is of no consequence, that he is ugly; give him but two hours with a woman, and he can destroy her. This beast is in full charge of the parish church of Parral, and had been transferred to that church because of complaints against him for seducing women.

"Another cura came one night to a house where two young men were visiting two young ladies. He called the young ladies to sit one each side, and spreading a manto in front of the three, began under the manto to handle the girls. The young men saw him do it, and had not spunk enough to kick the drunken rake out of doors. The mothers do not seem to make much objection to such actions. The mothers know of the unhappy relations of the priests with their daughters, and say nothing.

"In Cauquenes, the other day, a young woman ran into the chancel, just after the priest had consecrated the wine, and was about to drink it. She snatched the chalice from his hands, and in the presence of the congregation shouted, 'You are a bad man, and not worthy to drink that cup,' and at the word she drank the wine herself. The next Sunday she was in her place in the choir and nothing was done to her; though she had done a deed that would have put her in prison. But the priest retired from the church and went somewhere else. The parents of the young woman say, she was justified in this act. The account was published one week ago in *El Sur*, a paper of Concepcion. It was not long ago that the Bishop of Concepcion was the cause of the ruin of a young woman of high parentage: the facts were known to all Concepcion, but the Bishop still served. The mouths of friends were hushed. The bishop has since died of cholera. A gentleman in La Serena told me of the fact that a servant girl in his house was found in the family-way, and the author of her shame was an official member of the Bishop's house.

"This gentleman went to the Bishop and had the delinquent discovered and transferred to some other part. Had the child been born alive, it was his intention to make the priest support it.

"When after a long vacancy the present archbishop was called to fill the See, at the installation or consecration, a woman was observed to hold a child of two years up above the crowd, and was heard say to it, "That man [the new archbishop] is your father." She was followed to her house, and it was discovered that she was indeed a mistress of the high functionary. This account was published, and the address of the one who noted the fact given, yet no notice was taken of it. Not a single Roman Catholic paper said a word or referred to it; much less uttered an indignant denial, and demanded proof, or the punishment of the slanderer.

135

"Your book covers a wider ground, and deals also with fundamental questions in such a way that we would see it in the hands of every intelligent Romanist, and for this reason have written you.

I am,
J. M. ALLIS.
Santiago, Chili, S. A., May 4th, 1888. Casilla 912.

While it may not be wise to do more than has been attempted in "Why Priests Should Wed," it does seem important that the truth be given to the men and women of this Western world, that they may judge truly the character of Romanism, the life-long foe of morality, of virtue, and of Christianity.

12

Connubial Felicity Enjoyed by Priests and Nuns

IT IS IDLE TO DREAM of the purity of men who are accustomed to mouth words full of vile suggestions. "As a man thinketh, so is he." This had been theory. When the lecture entitled:

"NUNNERIES, PRISONS, OR WORSE,"

was delivered in one of our great cities, a storm of opposition was raised by Rome. The lecture was called "foul-mouthed" by leading Roman Catholics, and the nuns were spoken of as immaculate and above suspicion. A lady who had been ten years in one of the nunneries of the town, came to a subsequent lecture, and sent a friend to the platform of the crowded hall, who said: "I am authorized by a lady now in this audience, a member of a Congregational church"—giving her name, and the locality where she resided—"to say, that she has been ten years in a convent in this city, and for eight years wore the black veil as a nun; and she declares that all that has been said, charging incontinency upon priests and nuns, is true, but that the half has not been told." That was much. This that follows is more.

A gentleman occupying a distinguished position in the Christian world, brought the following statement. It seemed incredible, and was not used until it had been attested on oath. With feelings bordering on horror, it was read word for word; and if after reading this, that is faithfully copied, and the chapter preceding, there are those who claim that Romanism is worthy of regard, should they not be classed with those who gladly "believe a lie that they may be damned"?

A young man of seventeen years is walking the deck of an excursion steamer. Two men, dressed as priests, are on the deck. One of them bows to the young man. He returns the salutation. Whereupon one of the priests steps up and says: "I am glad, my son, to note your reverence for the fathers of your church." I said: "My custom is to treat with respect any professed teacher of Christian truth." He asked me to sit down beside him, and he enquired my name, age, occupation, parentage, purpose in life, etc.; and on my telling him that I expected to study law, he gave me much sound and wholesome advice. Finally he asked me if I knew him. I said: "No." He said he was His Grace the Archbishop of Toronto; and that the priest who was with him was Father. I expressed my due recognition of the honor of a conversation with His Grace; whereupon he said, he had taken quite an interest in me, and would like to grant me an absolution for my past sins, if I would confess them to him; and that he had no doubt he could get the key of the Captain's stateroom for the purpose. I replied that it would be useless, because I had no faith in the efficacy of any such pardoning.

He asked me to take off my hat and pray with him; and the three of us removed our hats, and he offered up a very earnest, brief prayer there upon the deck—the place where we were sitting being quite secluded, and we remained sitting during the prayer. After the prayer, he continued talking to me for an hour, giving me excellent advice on my life and habits, especially warning me against the gratification of sensual passions, either by self-abuse or harlotry.

From the steamboat they pass to a parlor-car; and there, the door being locked, the youth was asked to make himself comfortable on a couch at the side of the Archbishop. He then led the conversation into special lines. For example, he asked me: "If in school I had not often had my passion aroused by the legs of the girls being visible below their short dresses, and if I had not known boys who were seated across the aisle from the girls to deliberately drop pencils or books on the floor, so that, when picking them up, they might look under the skirts of the nearest girl." This is surprising language for an Archbishop to address to a youth of seventeen. It is but the prelude to the nastiness that follows.

This was one of the illustrations upon which he built skilful and forcible arguments against the Protestant public school question.

As a further illustration—this time on the line of the open Bible—he referred to Luke 1:23: "Every male that openeth the womb, shall be called holy to the Lord;" and he said that he knew of hundreds of instances where young men had twisted that passage into an excuse for immoral connection. And upon this, and other illustrations of a like nature, he erected what he thought an impregnable barrier against the free use of the Bible, apart from priestly guidance.

The Archbishop having attempted to awaken distrust in the mind of the youth in regard to the most pertinent and solid grounds of Protestantism, very quickly developed "a careful, elaborate and attractive description of the Roman Catholic Church, its universality, the grandeur of its history, its glorious ritual, its magnificent conquests in the past, the sanctity of a priest's life, the unequaled advantages for study which it offered, the high positions which faithful energy could achieve within its bounds, and particularly did he dilate on the opportunities which there were given for a complete education, a finished course of knowledge."

He dazzled me with a glorious view of Catholic scholarship, claiming that all truth lay within the reach of a priest, while the wonderful statement which he made of their communion with God seemed to clothe them with a halo of divinity. They were said to be above truth, because they were the companions of God, who was the Author of truth.

His portraiture of the Pope was dazzling. He was the monarch of emperors; his subjects were numbered by hundreds of millions. He was infallible, and the authorized representation of the Godhead on earth; and his treasures, whether viewed financially in gold and silver and precious stones, or spiritually in the worship given to him by his subjects—in any light, his treasures were infinite ; and this, he said, was possible to me, though, of course, not probable. *But he pointed out to me, that in the lawful struggle for ascendancy in the Catholic Church, my ambition could be satiated to its fullest fruition, and the greatest glory of my proudest desires could be more than satisfied;* while even if I never became more than a common priest, my power and influence would be far greater than that of the highest judge in the land; and all these glorious possibilities would be laid open to me then and there, *if I would but humbly and penitently become a convert to the truth.* I could go straight to Toronto with him, and within twenty-four hours could be safely under the fold of the only and everlasting church of God.

The triune oath required of me, he said, was very simple. *Poverty, chastity, and obedience* were then described; and so skilfully was the web laid that he thought my entanglement was complete.

It was at this juncture that I expressed my fear that, with my passionate nature, I could not keep pure the second vow, and that I had a great dislike to any pursuit in life that would quench the fire of my passion. This, I candidly stated to him, was a most serious obstacle; whereupon he gave me the following explanation of the vow, stating that it followed and was intimately connected with the first vow, and could be only thoroughly understood in that light; and that " when these two vows were properly understood, it was quite consistent with them that *the priest and the nun should mutually gratify the sensual desires of the other.* "

FIRST ARGUMENT.

(1) All priests and nuns must take the vow of poverty. (2) This vow means, the yielding to the service of the church of God, not only your property, but your body and your mind; that is to say, your affections and your very thoughts. (3) Therefore, you, as a person, no longer exist; both priest and nun are an inherent part of the church. (4) Hence, physical coition between the two was no more sin than the contact of the opposite organs of an hemaphrodite, or the mingling of the various robes of priest and nun — it was simply the contact of various parts of the one organization.

SECOND ARGUMENT.

(1) The Church was the bride of Christ. (2) The priest was the representative or local vicar of Christ. (3) It followed, that every nun, by

140

her marriage with the Church, became a part of the body of Christ's bride. (4) Hence, physical connection between priest and nun is not only the privilege, but becomes the duty, of those connected with the church.

THIRD ARGUMENT.

(1) The Word of God, and especially the epistles of Paul, particularly insist and teach, that every believer in Christ, becomes an organ in the body of Christ. (2) Hence, all members of the true Church of Christ become equal members of the one body. (3) Hence, as stated by Paul, in 1 Cor. 11: 21," The head cannot say to the feet, I have no need of thee." So neither can the priest or nun. (4) Hence, it follows again, as laid down by Paul in the same chapter, "that there should be no schism in the body, but that the members should have the same care one for another." (5) Hence, he concluded, that the coition of priest and nun for mutual comfort, was as natural as the chafing together of the right and left hand in cold weather.

The Archbishop was ably seconded in the matter by Father , whose role appeared to be the inserting of complimentary remarks concerning the Archbishop, and extolling his wisdom, learning, zeal, etc.

After this came the suggestion that the young man should leave gun and rod in the passenger coach, and drop his hat out of the window; which would lead his parents to believe that he had fallen from the train; while the non-discovery of his body would always remain with them as a hope that he was not dead and might ultimately return; while he was to proceed with the Archbishop to the city, where, after being admitted into the Catholic Church, he would be provided with a first-class passage to Rome, and a recommendation to an eminent official there; from which time onward, all the scholarships of Christendom would be within his grasp, while the only limits to his towering ambition would be the energy and ability which he should display to entitle him to it, and the fullest gratification of all natural desires could be accomplished in a manner perfectly consistent with a holy and sanctified life, the service of Christ and his fellow-men, with the certain guarantee of eternal life.

Such was the Archbishop's scheme. If anything more devilish can be devised, it proves great capacity in that line. The youth was earnestly persuaded not to reject the truth. See him! He is in the car without a friend. The Archbishop and priest are his keepers. All knelt together in prayer. The prelate prayed for his conversion. A few minutes might have sealed his doom; when, in the mercy of God, the locomotive's shrill whistle blew for his home station. That sudden shriek brought him back suddenly to reality and decision. One thought of home, of mother, of Bible and Christ, and the temptation was gone. Thanking the Archbishop for his kindness, he sprung to the door, turned the key, retired from the car, and in a moment was upon the platform — saved from popery and hell!

Does such a statement throw any light upon the conduct of priests? Is it strange that men thus taught so often fall? "Oh," said a young priest to Blanco White, with tears in his eyes, after having for four or five years discharged the duties of his station, "God only knows what I have suffered during this time! And if I have fallen, it is not without fighting. Had I been allowed to choose a wife—as it is the law of God, who destines man to marriage, whatever our rules teach to the contrary,—I should have been the happiest man in the world; I should be a good, a holy priest; while now, I am—oh, I am ashamed of myself!" This is really the sad history of all their falls; for, let us be just, no men are tempted like priests. Their passions are often necessarily aroused. The demon of bad thoughts takes possession of them. Their ministry drives them into such relations with women, into whose most secret thoughts they are obliged to enter, that their virtue receives many shocks. Admit that in the beginning they try to be faithful. They flutter, fall, reform again, go on, fall again, and at length, to finish this horrible struggle, abandon faith, and sink into Atheism; because of the impossibility of reconciling their faith with conduct so vile, and yet so common to the class.

If the statement of the Archbishop contains the truth, what a horrid light it sheds upon the conduct of priests!

A gray-haired mother who had fled from Rome to Christ, came and said: "My granddaughter is being wooed and won by Father." She spoke as if the priest was a lover, and not a minister.

"Can priests win hearts? Is that their vocation?"

"They were nominally for the church; but really for themselves," was the sad reply.

They had read "Why Priests Should Wed," and were startled by its terrible revelations. The young lady accompanied her grandmother to the house of God. Beautiful in face and form, attractive in manner, soft-toned in speech, she seemed fitted to make some man a good wife, and to become the centre of a pleasant home. She had determined to become a nun. The cloister was not in her thought, nor was religion. She was in love with the priest, and thought of passing into the cloister that she might have him, so soon as she became a spiritual sister. Then came Gavazzi's words of warning to the nun. He said: "The Jesuits, too, have nuns. For almost every order of monks there is a corresponding order of nuns. If monks are useless and dangerous, what are nuns? They are very gentle-speaking ladies, very delicate ladies; but, are they Scriptural? No! Christ never instituted nuns! He came alike to men and women, and all the human race. Among his followers were humble and devout women, Mary Magdalen and Martha and others, to whom he spoke of things eternal; but did he ever say to any of them: 'I wish you to become a nun?' Never! He said: 'Come and follow me;' but never, 'Go to a cloister!'* And yet nuns swarm in Washington. They ride in carriages; they walk in procession; they fatten at the public crib, and are treated by Congressmen as if they were worthy of supreme regard. Their names we need not give, nor describe the great establishment. Do parents understand, in the light of the Archbishop's statement, the character, standing, and habits of these "Sisters" so-called, who with the gratification of every passionate desire are promised eternal life?

It is time the iniquitous character of these institutions were made known. If nuns are what the Archbishop describes them, the mistresses of priests, let it be known.

---

* Gavazzi's Lectures, pp. 87.

Do parents consider the terrible meaning of the conduct of a priest when he makes love to a girl and obtains her consent to abandon home and friends, and immure herself in a convent, and become in her full maturity, in her ripe beauty, the slavish subject of the priest?

In "Why Priests Should Wed," the warnings of Wm. Hogan and Maria Monk are given, but the words of the Archbishop, and the argument by which the position is maintained, throw light upon this subject. As educators, nuns are failures. They live under the influence of their father-confessors. These are generally Jesuits, or Jesuitically educated; the nun will impart to her pupil the same education she receives from her spiritual director,—a poor, bigoted, contemptible, anti-American education. This is the education given by those nunned and cloistered teachers, the willing subject of the priests, and who by example, if not by word, make a pretension to virtue a play, if not a by-word and a sham.

Beware for your homes. Nuns are to be found not only in monasteries, but abroad; they travel in disguise, like Jesuits. They enter homes as servants; and though often deemed a great blessing in a Protestant family, they are at times just the reverse. They know how to peep through the keyhole, and carry all information they can obtain to the father confessor. Would you have in your families an adroit, consummate spy? Take a servant educated by nuns, and your wish is gratified. It is beginning to be fashionable to think that hospitals and asylums are sure to be well cared for if given into the charge of Sisters of Charity. Before they were introduced, hospitals and schools were well attended; and were they now extinct, American institutions would be well cared for; while what good they do is more than outweighed by the unmitigated evil of the general aim and tendency of monastic institutions.

13

Jesuits In the Parlor; or, Fashionable Life In Washington

IT WOULD REQUIRE THE GENIUS of a Disraeli to do justice to the many-sided characteristics of fashionable life in Washington. More and more, throng there, during the winter months, the women of fashion and the men of note, who make Saratoga, Newport, and Long Branch places of attraction and repute during the summer. Washington is becoming a great winter resort. People come there, some for politics, some for office, some for patronage, and others for the rich pickings or plums of party favor bestowed by their representatives in the House and Senate, by the men whom they have been delighted to honor with their support at home, and who feel that obligation and interest alike, compel and command them to do for them all in their power to make their sojourn in Washington a delight.

The receptions at the White House, the spreads given by the members of the Cabinet and other officials of high life, foreign and home, furnish abundant entertainments to which entrance is not difficult, and is within the reach of the deserving. In fashionable life, are many citizens of Washington who understand etiquette, and are leaders and directors of the movements which bring pleasure or pain. Some ambitious relative of a distinguished official gets her name on the page of the Court paper, and becomes a ruling star. Round her gather lesser lights. Ambitious young men connected with the army or navy, with foreigners of distinction, or attaches of the ministers who represent foreign countries, rival the young Congressman, the son of a senator, or mayhap a President, or the bright and noble array of newspaper men, who hold in their hands the making or unmaking of reputations, the successful writer, orator, or financier, who are there with an eye to business, and are regarded as a great catch at home, and therefore as objects of regard abroad, share in the pleasures of the dance, chat at the supper, and play their part in the saloon of fashion, brilliant with light, and radiant with the corruscated rays flashing from brilliant diamonds worn in profusion by the attractive American women, who are becoming each year sought after by the titled and great of this and other lands. Among these are Jesuits, without the name, dressed in the height of fashion, capable of conversing in any tongue, and so able to bring together the Cuban and the pride of Paris, the German and the sweet-toned Italian; standing as an intermediate not only between different nationalities, but different sects and classes. They know life. They have influence with the great. They sport in the light of the Red-Robed Cardinal, who keeps his high place as prince of the church, and as ruler in the political world, to an extent little appreciated by the uninitiated. Ever on the watch to bring a Protestant of influence, or of wealth—which in Washington creates influence—into association with a Roman Catholic of prominence and position, it is not difficult to see that on this continent Washington opens to Romanism a field of richest possibilities. Beside them, and working with Brothers of the Order, are female Jesuits, as well-trained; distinguished for skill in diplomacy, in *finesse,* always ready to leave any ordinary occupation to further the interests of the church.

At their head for years and years, ranked that cultured and famed wife of a great general who wears on her breast the "Golden Rose," presented by the Pope of Rome. Associating with her are ladies who rank high in Evangelical associations, and who are always ready to accept a second or a subordinate place on boards of hospitals or homes; where they vote as they are bidden, and help to place power and patronage under the control of that one great organism which works parties, senates, and supreme courts, with an eye not to God's glory, but the good and growth of the party of Rome. As proof, read a few well-known facts.

It was at a magnificent party, a beautiful girl, on her father's arm, paused, and shook the hand of a distinguished gentleman whose prospects brightened every hour as the probable nominee for the presidency. He made a passing and complimentary remark, which brought a blush to the cheek, brightness to the eye, and a thrill of joy to the heart. Not far away stood a young man, the son of a Protestant, a student at Princeton, enamored of her beauty and glad to hear her praises spoken by one so highly esteemed. In a little time he was at her side. They were together evening after evening. Every hindrance was removed. Room was given them. Invitation followed invitation to places where pleasure reigned. There were those who saw the game and wished it well. The Jesuits were delighted. The President had placed the church of Rome under great obligations, by having his Secretary of State address a letter to the Italian government, asking that the American College be saved from confiscation. It was done; and the name of the President, as his own successor, was taken up on the-tongue of the press, and rolled like a sweet morsel for months. He deserved what was said of him. He was an honest, true, and good President, and proved that he was an exception to the rule, that a Vice-President succeeding to the presidency must be a traitor to the party who elected him.

It was thought that he could be used as an instrument in furthering a scheme upon which thought, money, and much planning had been bestowed. He, the son of a Baptist minister, had married an Episcopalian, and had been led by his wife into the more fashionable church, and was one of the most devout of worshippers. The Jesuits saw in that step but the beginning that might lead him into the fold of a church in which apostolic succession was a claimed verity, and not a pretence. Along this path thousands had marched into the embrace of Rome. Why not this cultured man? Up came the happy couple to this polite and clear-sighted man, who, handsome in face, faultless in dress, dignified in mien, and courteous in speech, is the centre of attraction.

As the young and happy couple pass, a friend to the President remarks: "A most desirable match!"

"She is a Roman Catholic," replied the President.

"What of that?" was the outspoken ejaculation, as a shadow of disappointment swept over the faces of the Jesuitical throng; "surely, that would not form an obstacle in the opinion of a gentleman who allowed his heart-love to rule so much of his life as was shown in his devotion to his wife."

The President's face flushed, and his eye flashed, as he replied: "It would make a vast difference. Between a girl professing faith in Christ and a member of the *Protestant* Episcopal Church, and a Roman Catholic, is a wide remove. Should the young man marry into that home, they will be compelled either to be married in a Roman Catholic church with its attendant display, or an altar must be built in the home, and the bridegroom must consent to having their offspring given up to the church of Rome. This would, in my opinion, be an inseparable barrier to the union."

A polite acquiescence was given.

In another part of the room was a hurried conversation. That woman distinguished in securing the advancement of any one connected with the Roman Catholic church, from a man who empties ash-barrels to one seeking a Cabinet appointment, spoke warmly and wisely: "Sound him. Find out if those are his views. If so, we will have done with him."

To the girl the words were recited. She would gladly have turned from Rome. She was tired of its empty mummeries, and longed for something better. These men, who know so well the weaknesses of women, knew how to manage her. She soon found herself fenced in to Jesuitical influences, and apart and away from Protestant associations.

A Jesuit took the young man to ride, and there learned that he would stand with his household—that he would not surrender to Rome.

The father of the girl, a devout Roman Catholic, believed he could remove the hindrance. The household quoted the words of the President in approval. To the President went the Congressman, assured of his power to carryall before him. The son of a Baptist minister, born in the north of Ireland, and knowing Romanism as it is, and hating it because of its deserts, was firm and decided. Archbishop, bishop, priest and Jesuit, tried to persuade, and finally to compel. In vain! Rome had reached a stone wall! It could not go over it. It was difficult to go around it! At this time the President was riding on the high and crested wave of popularity. A second term was an assured fact, in the estimation of the million. His name was on the world's broad tongue like the sound of the falling of a force. His praises filled the press, and rolled like a tide current over the world. He was honest, capable, industrious, and a mighty manipulator of men. His knowledge of the requirements of high life surpassed all his predecessors. As a club man, he was an authority; and as a referee in difficult cases, his decisions were marked by sound judgment and fairness, and were not appealed from. To break such a man, seemed like a herculean task; but the Jesuits said it should be done, if he did not bow to Rome.

The health of the young lady gave way. The Jesuits made the most of it. The father and the magnates of the church grew desperate. There was great commotion in fashionable life. Rome had never been baffled before. Could she be baffled now?

The Congressman, beaten and almost broken, took his daughter to his home, where she died, it is said, with a broken heart. This was as the Jesuits desired. Then came the organizing against the President, and in favor of a man more subtle, more complaisant, more ready to yield.

As was natural, thought turned towards a General of the army, the friend and companion of Grant, and the most popular man in Washington. His tall form; short, quick, nervous step; always well dressed, but never gaudily; a hater of new clothes, and of new ways; with an extraordinary head, big and full at the top; with a brain that had been too big for the body, had not the latter been developed into a bundle of iron tissues by the hardest of physical exertions,—he was a man to be pointed out as the commanding feature of any gathering. His "great campaigns, in which he generally slept on the ground without a tent, in the earlier part of his military career, gave him a constitution which served him well. His face was rough, and it had a strong expression. He was pat-tongued. Epigrams flew from it like sparks from an anvil. Though nominally a member of the church, he was noted for his profanity. He carried a cigar in his mouth almost as much as Grant. When he smokes he smokes all over, so to speak. He seems to be disgusted with his cigar, and sucks in its nicotine as though it was the hardest thing in the world to get it to draw. He brushes off the ashes with a quick, nervous gesture, and throws away the cigar when it is only half smoked. He uses the weed fully as much as any man in the army.

"The shape of his head was much discussed at the time it was alleged he was a lunatic. This was when he told Simon Cameron and Lorenzo Thomas that it would take 200,000 men to drive the rebels out of Kentucky. These two gentlemen laughed at the idea, and would not accept his advice concerning Kentucky. He then asked to be relieved. He was ordered elsewhere, and another took his place. This was on November 30, 1861; and on the same night, the report that he was crazy was sent out by a correspondent of one of the New York papers.

"During the first part of Andrew Jackson's term he lived in the family of Senator ——, at ——, O., a sleepy country-town of perhaps a couple of thousand inhabitants, where the boys loafed about the stores and listened to the older loafers tell stories. His comrades called him 'Gump,' and one of them says he was among the laziest of them, and that he could always be found at the stores of an evening. 'He was a different fellow,' says this gentleman, 'from ——, who was a great reader, and a sort of plodder. 'Gump' had a great idea of going to West Point, and he talked of it continually. I shall never forget the day his uncle finally got him his appointment. He was so happy he could hardly contain himself, and he almost walked on the air for several days.

"He graduated at the early age of 20, and entered the artillery, serving first in the Florida war, as first lieutenant during the Mexican war, in California as adjutant-general. Ten years after he graduated he married his patron's daughter, who was then Secretary of the Interior, and the wedding came off in grand style at Washington. Clay, Webster, Calhoun and Tom Benton were all present, as was also the President and his cabinet. He was thirty years old then. His beard was a dingy red, and he had a face bronzed with service in the West. The couple went to New York, Niagara Falls, and then to Washington. He stayed in the army three years after his marriage; but in 1853 resigned, and went to San Francisco, where he opened a broker's shop. He afterward had a bank at No. 12 Wall Street, New York City. But neither of these ventures could have paid very well; for very shortly after, we find he left for Kansas, where his brothers-in-law were practising at the bar.

"His family are missed, in a social way, for the general was the life of many a dinner table. He lived very nicely here, in a three-story building, on — street, very near the White House, Wormley's Hotel, and the Riggs. Here he had an office in the basement, where you could find him at odd hours working away. At the War Department he was, perhaps, the most busy man in the great building. He seemed to be always going at lightning speed. In his eyes the department clerk was as good as the long-winded United States senator, and if he were in a good humor, the clerk would be just as well received. If he were in a bad humor—and this was by no means uncommon—both had better keep away. This quality of the general has tended much to the good of the army. Military men, especially of the lower orders, are inclined to pomp and snobbery. His blunt, off-hand ways, his plain, practical ideas, and his bold way of calling a spade, a spade, has done much to foster common sense among the military men here.

"His habit of sometimes letting his feelings carry him away came near being his ruin in the days following the accession of Andrew Johnson. Johnson, you know, repudiated his agreement with Joe Johnston at the time, though he afterwards practically adopted it. One of the leading war correspondents of the time tells the story. He says:

"Sullen at the repudiation of his agreement with Johnston, angry at the interference of Gen. Halleck with the co-operative movements of himself and, furious at the countermanding of his orders by the Secretary of War, he marched to Washington with his army, breathing vengeance upon Halleck, and hate and contempt upon Stanton. No nation safely before witnessed such a spectacle—a victorious general, at the head of 80,000 men devoted to him and jealous of his fame as a part of their own, marching to the capital of the country, with threats against his military superiors breathing from his lips and flowing from his pen. For days he raved around Washington, expressing his contempt for Halleck and Stanton in the strongest terms, and denouncing them as mere non-combatants whom he despised. He wrote to his friends, and through them to the public, comparing Halleck and Stanton to cowardly Falstaffs, seeking to win honor for the deeds he had done, accusing the Secretary of War of suppressing his reports and endeavoring to slander him before the American public in official bulletins. For days his army roamed the streets of the capital with the same freedom with which they had roamed through the fields of war, and no man dared to raise his voice in condemnation of their leader or approval of the superiors who had opposed him. No Republic ever was in such danger before, and yet the danger was hardly suspected.

"This affair, however, blew over, and he never was called to account for his actions. No record was made of the offense against discipline, which in any other country would have cost him, not merely his position, but his reputation, and in many armies his life. Still, in all this he never meditated anything against the Government and never forgot his allegiance."*

The timber out of which to make a President was clearly in this mm. The wife being approached was not averse to whatever might give power to the church, and so readily yielded consent. It was believed that the manner in which the father had surrendered his idolized son to the Romish priesthood, was an indication of his readiness to yield compliance to their demands.

He was in St. Louis when the proposition was broached. "It won't do," replied the great General. "My wife is a Roman Catholic, and most devoted to the interests of the church. That is enough. The country would never give its support to a man who, when elected, would be compelled to see the White House overrun with priests." That outspoken man was abandoned.

There was another ready. A man born a Roman Catholic, converted to the Protestant faith, professedly, and having united with the Congregational church, and having a wife devoted to Christian work, moving in the first circles, seemed to be fitted, if it could be managed.

There was much in his favor. His relatives were all Roman Catholics. His mother died in the church, and he had said that for a

---

* Frank G. Carpenter, in Special Correspondence.

"dozen presidencies, he would not *say* a word against the religion of his mother." His two sisters were at the head of two convents. His brother was a devout Romanist, and it was said that his father died in that faith. In the town and much in society, was a man sixty years of age, who was noted for wearing on his breast a medal given him by Pio Nono, because he belonged to his Pontifical Guard.

THE JESUITS, MALE AND FEMALE,

Turn to this man as suited to their plan. He is introduced into the family of the senator. He becomes acquainted with the daughter. Barriers are removed. The way is open. Marriage is proposed. The daughter joins the Roman Catholic church, and an altar is built in the home, and the "medal" soldier of Pio Nono marries the daughter of the most magnetic man of the age.

At once his name is taken up. Banners are worked for him. *"The dividing of the Irish vote"* is spoken of as a desirable result. Here is a man, born a Roman Catholic, and becoming a Protestant, and yet supported by Romanists for the Presidency. Is not that a proof that in this land there is no danger from Rome? That Romanists can separate church State, and vote for a man who left them, and yet not so bigoted as to oppose them? It seemed as if the American people were dead to apprehension. The Pope was spoken of as a well-meaning gentleman. Romanists in high positions began to be consulted by politicians. The bargain was made. The goods were not delivered. Never was a more propitious time to act. The guns of Protestantism were still. In all the land, with here and there an exception, those who had fought Romanism had grounded arms. Romanism was a menace, no more. From every altar the nominee was praised, and tickets were given to the faithful to be deposited in the ballot box.

WHY WAS HE NOT ELECTED?

There is but one answer: *God* was against the sale. At a great reception, which was claimed to be a spontaneous outpouring of the

153

ministry connected with the Evangelical denominations, to offset any fear arising from the statement which was going abroad, *that the proposition had been made to the Vicar-Generals of the Archbishop of New York and Brooklyn, "Give me the Roman Catholic vote, and I will do for Romanism what has never been done before."*

So the ministry came from far and near. The gentleman expected to deliver the address was called away. The Rev. Dr. Burchard was invited to take his place. He was an old man, given to alliterations. He said, in a low voice, so low that few heard it,—"We are Republicans, and don't propose to leave our party and identify ourselves with the party whose antecedents have been Rum, Romanism and Rebellion."

A reporter of the *Press* overheard these words, took them down, sold what he claimed would defeat the Republican and elect the Democratic candidate, and having pocketed his money, gave them wing.

The words were caught up and flashed over the world. Had the nominee said, That is true, all would have been well. Why did he not say it? He could not! Behind him was the altar, the giving away of his child, the bargain, the Jesuit host all about, the demand that he prove himself true to Rome, however false he might be to the principles professed when he turned from Rome and gave himself professedly to Christ. The next day it was printed; and he said: *"For a dozen presidencies, I would not say a word against the religion of my mother."* Why not? If the religion of his mother was so bad that he decided he ought to turn from it, it was so bad that it ought to be opposed, no matter who professed it.

Defeat came. Why? One paper called it "bad luck." The candidate said, "It was because it rained;" and other excuses were given.

Was it "bad luck," or *God?* It is a question which Americans will do well to answer.

On the deck of an ocean steamer, men discuss the probable chances of prominent men for the presidency. Among them is a Jesuit, who keeps his own counsel. Just opposite the Never Sink, as they approach the harbor of New York, the Jesuit asks one who has been foremost in the discussion, "Do you know who selects your President?"

"The people," was the swift reply.

"No!"

"Who?"

"The Pope of Rome. Everyman who succeeds has to have his endorsement."

"My friend," said the politician, "your words remind me of a story. A Quaker friend was in conversation with a neighbor who was addicted to falsehood. One day, when he had told a whopper, he said:

'Friend A——, I do not like to call thee a liar, but if the Mayor of Philadelphia should ask me to show him the greatest liar I ever knew, I would go to thee and say, 'Friend A——, the Mayor wants to see thee.' And so, sir, though I would not like to call you a liar, this I will say, never was a man more mistaken. Let it be known whom Rome wants, and the American people will want and have the other man, and the history of our late conflict proves it. Rome may conspire against, and perhaps defeat, but cannot elect. She may hinder, but cannot control."

"As an illustration, who is more popular than this man? For whom was such a welcome ever prepared? True, Rome did her best, and pulled the wires well, and the menials who do her bidding thought to throw the nominee of the party into the shade, and foist this man to the chief place again; but once more a power they could not control took charge of affairs. Seventy-five thousand people looked and waited; some of them tossed on the waves grew sick and weary, and he did not come. The play came on with Hamlet left out, and once more the Hand which wrote on the palace-wall, *"Mene, mene, tekel, apharsin,"* appeared, the plan was marred, and the scheme was ruined.

Will this teach the people that it is safe to be true? Jesuitism is potent, but not all-potent. God Almighty has managed the affairs of this world a good while. As a result, the Pope is a prisoner in the Vatican, and Romanism needs only to be exposed to be expurgated from the plans of politics, and the purpose of this great free nation.

14

A Warning and an Appeal; or, The Huguenots, Their Folly and Their Fall

SHALL AMERICANS CONTEND FOR THE truth or betray it? This is the question of this hour, and of all hours.

Men are created for God's glory. God does not waste his time or energies in holding up and blessing those who refuse to glorify him. He gives them up. He lets go of them. If they insist on going to the Devil, to the Devil they go, and make out of it what they can.

It is a glorious privilege to know God. It is the manifest duty of those who know him to be thankful for the knowledge, and to use it wisely and well. Whoever fails to do this, makes a loss. The Huguenots, in their folly and their fall, illustrate this truth. There was a time when those who professed the religion of Jesus Christ were in the majority in France. Then they had an open Bible, a Sabbath sacred to holy uses, the wealth, the culture and the government. They lost all because they did not champion and proclaim the truth God had intrusted to their care.

When Henry IV., in 1598, issued the Edict of Nantes, and acknowledged God, and evidenced his gratitude by giving to Christianity, as taught by the Gospel, a place in the lives, thoughts and plans of men, he enriched France.

When Louis XIV., in 1685, revoked the Edict of Nantes, and gave his country over to the black-hearted villainy and terrible despotic hate of Romanism, to be despoiled and degraded, he brought ruin upon the State, and eternal infamy upon his name.

Then France was taken off the list of God-fearing States, and was enveloped in night, shrouded in superstition, that begets ignorance, poverty and death. In 1537 there were eight hundred and six churches in

France. A bright future awaited them. France has known three periods in her religious life. Let us name them:

1. The Period of Repression, 1512-1559.

The attempt was made to reform the Papal church. It was in vain. As well might the attempt be made to clean out sin. It is ours to come out from it, and bring others out. This we can do. It is what men are within that makes them. It is what Romanists believe that damns them. The cry should be, "Come out from her, my people, that ye be not partakers of her sins." Protestants hoped that error unrebuked would be dispersed by the truth. This is the dream of thousands in America. It is a false dream, built on a false hope.

2. The Period of Organization, 1559-1562.

This was the hour of battle. The Huguenots flamed as torch-bearers for Christ Jesus. The ministry and nobility revealed courage, and as the churches followed, effective work was done for God.

3. The Period of Resistance, 1559-1662.

This period deserves a book rather than a paragraph. Figures, some fearless and uncompromising, others devilish and malignant, are on the stage. Gaspard de Coligni, Charlotte Laval, Jeanne d'Albert, mother of Navarre, how grandly they stand forth for God and the right!

Over against them are, Charles IX., Catherine de Medici, Alva, the Duke of Guise and others, whose deeds blacken the page of history. See them at work! "Bring out the books and burn them," is the savage demand of the Duke of Guise, as he reins up his horse in front of the barn where 3,000 have gathered to hear Leonard Morel as he preaches Christ.

"In whom do you believe?" is the question asked of the watchman at the door. "In the Lord Jesus Christ," is the brave answer. "Cut him down." "Dogs, rebels, Huguenots, heretics," are the appellations thrown at the worshippers of Christ. The watchman is slain. Leonard Morel is struck with a musket. He falls on his knees and prays for his enemies. *"Bring out the book!"* The Bible is handed him. He opens and looks at the date. "This the Bible? It is 1500 years and more since this book was written. It was printed within a year." Wonderful truth! The Bible is old and yet new! Huguenot was, at the onset, a term of reproach. Afterwards, it became an honor. About the origin of the name there are various legends.

Davila finds a derivation for the name in the fact that they worshipped in cellars near Hugo's gate. Others declare, the name came from Hugh Capet, from whom they claimed descent. It was not his origin, but his deeds, that made the Huguenot a power.

He has been described as a "soldier with the Testament in his knapsack, the Psalms on his lips, the name of Jehovah on his banner, the conviction of the Divine Presence as his leader"—that made him a power.

On the field of battle the vision of liberated France was ever before his eye. His enemies were the enemies of God, who began each new war for the Papal idolatries. He fought them for Christ's sake, and fired each shot with a prayer, and saw with thanksgiving a routed foe. He rushed to the charge without fear; lie cut right and left with unsparing severity; he made it his work until the order was given to desist. He held every truce and treaty sacred. He had mercy for the prisoner, the maimed and the dying. He forgave as generously as he fought grievously. He boasted not of his own valor, if he was the conqueror; he had no despair if be was the vanquished. He murmured not if he must die for Christ and country. He gave his soul to God, expected his pockets to be rifled, his body left for the eagles, and his bones to bleach under a sun that might yet shine upon a liberated kingdom.

"Honest as a Huguenot," was the proverb coined in his honor and made current through long generations, because of what he was when he was at his best—God's child, fearless for the truth, the foe of Romanism, the champion of liberty, at any cost or sacrifice.

Gaspard d'Coligni was the flower grown on the stem of a Huguenot's faith. He was born Feb. 16, 1517, at Chatillon sur Laing. He came from good stock. His father was a brave soldier and an incorruptible patriot. He trained Gaspard to be brave. There were three boys, who loved each other, Odet, Gaspard and Francis. The star of the Reformation shone in the mother's heart. The senior, Gaspard, chief marshal of the army, while hastening to relieve a beleaguered town, became overheated and died. He made a will commending wife and children to the king and brother-in-law Montmorency, and died on the ninth day of his illness.

The grief of the fatherless lads found some solace in their mother's love, and in their affection for each other. Whoever was loved by the one was loved by the other two, and whoever offended one had an affair to settle with the entire three.

The mother of Coligni, in the home of Margaret Navarre, became the governess of Jeanne d' Albert, the mother of Henry IV. It is probable that she made much of the friendship of this wonderful woman, who, for diversion, read the Holy Scriptures, saying, " In perusing them, my mind experiences its true and perfect joy." His uncle was a rough soldier.

Coligni's conversion to Christ was the foundation of his strength. It was in the castle at Ghent, while a prisoner, that he received a copy of the Scriptures, while on the brink of the grave. Audelot his brother, a prisoner at the same time, was released because he permitted the mass to be said in his cell. Coligni paid his ransom, and retired to his castle at Chatillon. There Charlotte Laval, his good wife, became his teacher. When urged to profess Christ, he replied:

"It is wise to count the cost of being a true Christian."

"It is wiser to count the cost of not being a true Christian. In the one case, the cost is temporal. In the other, it is eternal. In the one, the body pays it; but in the other, the soul pays it for ever."

"You are right," replied the Admiral, "and if you are ready for the sacrifice, so am I;" and from that time he professed the reformed creed. He gave the Scriptures to his servants, forbade profane swearing, engaged pious teachers for his children, and established schools among the poor. One day, being at Vaterille, listening to the word of God, the truth broke in upon his mind. He then saw that the true preparation for the Supper is not in the elements used, but in the person using them; he must have faith in Christ. It was then he came into the full fellowship of the church.

The influence of this act was felt far and wide.

Happy for France if there had been a John Knox at the head of the Reform,—a man bold in the face of royalty, scathing upon usurpers, reading the tendency of political schemes, so that he could march abreast of events, the standard-bearer of the truth!

The Reform-movement went on. Churches multiplied. A fourth of the kingdom became identified with the churches of Christ.

The uprising of the *Huguenots* called for Coligni. He hesitated. His wife knew the struggle in his soul. She could not sleep. She thought of them enjoying every blessing in the palace, while their brethren were in dungeons, or on the bare fields with the storm beating on them. He urged that war might only increase the number of the sufferers. "Your argument leaves your brethren hopeless. It does not show a strong faith in God," said the good wife. "He has given you the genius of a great Captain. You have confessed the jnstice [*sic*] of their cause." "Lay your hand on your heart, wife, and tell me: Could you receive the news of defeat without a murmur against God, and a reproach upon your husband?"

"I could." "Are you prepared to see your husband branded as a rebel and dragged to a scaffold, while your children are disgraced and begging their bread of their enemies, or serving them as scullions and slaves? I give you eight days to reflect upon it, and if you are prepared for such reverses, I will march." "The eight days are already expired," said the intrepid wife. "Go sir, where duty calls." He went. We cannot follow him. From camp to cabinet; from cabinet to camp: now wounded, now defeated, but always undaunted, he went forth, until August 24, 1572, when, on the night of St. Bartholomew, he was murdered while a guest of the king; his body thrown from the window to the ground, had its head severed, and then was placed upon a gibbet; afterward his body having been dragged about the streets, put over a fire and scorched, and thrown into the river, taken out again as unworthy food for fish, dragged again by boys and lewd fellows of the baser sort, was hung up again on the gallows, feet upward, where it remained for two weeks.

All this, and volumes more, was the background of 1637.

Now, look forward. Dark grows the night because God's children withhold the light. Bright grows the day whenever the messengers of Christ have the courage of their convictions.

So long as the Huguenots filled out in their lives, and by their proclamation of the truth, the conception which the world still cherishes of them, they prospered.

Henry IV. illustrates, in his life and in his death, the uselessness of cowardice. He had courage on the battlefield, a rough wit, and in some circumstances would have shone as a leader. But in that age he lacked the faith which was essential to victory. He did not see Him who is invisible. His life was not built on Christ, the corner stone. The trial came. He was weighed in the balance and *"Mene, mene, tekel, upharsin,"* was as true of him as of Belshazzar. He was found wanting in steadfastness of purpose. He surrendered to Rome when a lad. He dared not be a Daniel. He trifled when he should have been resolute and firm. Brave and skillful in war, he lost the advantage of his splendid victories by trying to serve both parties. At last, he tore himself treacherously from the faith of his mother, and from all the associations of his early years. On the 25th of July, 1593, he knocked on Sunday morning at the Cathedral of St. Dennis. The door was opened, and upon the bishop demanding his errand, he replied, "To he admitted into the church of Rome." He bowed at the altar, and swore allegiance to the Roman faith. He acted a lie. He thought the throne of France worth a mass, and consented, because Rome would not assent to his ruling on any other conditions, to become a godless king. He had asked once before, "Could you confide in the faith of an atheist? And in the day of battle would it add to your courage to think you followed the banner of a perjured apostate?" Brave words, had he followed them; but he surrendered, and lost all. The Rome he sought to placate, turned from him with fresh aversion in 1598, when he issued the Edict of Nantes, twenty-six years after the massacre of St. Bartholemew. The essence of the edict was limited toleration. Liberty of conscience was permitted to the Huguenots; but except in special parts of France, they could not exercise their religion. They were declared eligible to office. Their poor were admitted into the hospitals; but they were required to keep the Romish festivals and pay tithes. For a time the edict was observed, and under its shelter the Huguenots pursued their way, enjoying a measure of quiet and liberty. Then, had they preached the truth, they might have achieved a victory. But they suppressed it. They lacked the courage which was displayed by Antonio Court, who gathered little crowds about him, and went on until there were thousands listening to his voice.

The History of French Protestantism from the promulgation of the Edict of Nantes, by Henry IV., in 1598, to the revocation of the same edict by Louis XIV., in 1685, naturally divides itself into three periods. In the first, extending from that great religious transaction which marks the end of the civil wars of the sixteenth century, to the taking of Rochelle in 1629, the Protestants were at one time by their own fault, and at another by the artifice of the nobles, involved in the troubles which agitated the regency of Maria de Medici; and in the first years of the majority of Louis XII., beheld themselves deprived of the fortresses or towns yielded to them in pledge for the fulfillment of treaties of their political organization, and of their influence in the State.

Had they resisted this inroad, they could have held Romanism in check. But when the Huguenots allowed a solemn compact to be trifled with, Rome believed her hour had come, and marched boldly on.

God gives every body a chance. Accept it, and salvation is assured. Reject it, and all is lost.

In the second period (1629-1662), which extends from the taking of Rochelle to the first persecutions of Louis XIV., the Protestants lived as Protestants in America are trying to live. They surrendered their influence as a religious party. Their chiefs pulled down the banner of a protest against the aggressions of Rome and sought for quiet and prosperity and thrift.

They disturbed France no longer, as their ancestors had done, by incessant armed risings, but enriched themselves by their industry.

FOR A TIME THEY PROSPERED.

Deprived of their cautionary fortresses and of their political organizations, gradually excluded from employment at Court and from nearly all civil offices, they turned to agriculture and to manufactures, and amassed fortunes. They redeemed lost provinces from sterility.

The Protestant burgher-class in the towns applied itself to industry and commerce, and displayed a degree of activity and intelligence coupled to integrity such as never have been surpassed in any country. In Guienne it nearly monopolized the wine trade; in the two governments of Brouoge and Oleron, a dozen Protestant families held a monopoly of the trade in salt and wine which amounted yearly to twelve or fifteen million livres.

Those of Cæn, sold to English and Dutch merchants linen and clothes manufactured at Vive, at Falouse, and at Argenton; thus securing a rich outlet for this branch of national industry. Though bad Catholics, Romanists were compelled to admit that the Reformed were excellent men of business.

Swamped by a ruinous legislation to which they assented, and tolerated in the midst of a population entirely outnumbering them, which ever regarded them with suspicion, constantly the butt of all calumnies, subjected to the control of imperious laws which compelled them to exercise perpetual constraint upon themselves, they forced public esteem by their austerity of morals and irreproachable loyalty. By the confession of their enemies, they respected law, they obeyed God, loved their fellowmen, and were true to them. They lived as seeing Him who is invisible. "Renowned for their commercial intelligence and activity, they were no less famous for their industry. More devoted to labor than other subjects of the realm, because they could only hope to equal them by surpassing them in the quality of their work, they were

still further stimulated and advanced by the principles of their religion."
Those principles forbid their inaction in thought. Compelled to
enlighten themselves by diligent study, there came necessarily the
superior light, which spread itself over all their actions, and rendered
their spirit abler to grasp all ideas the application of which would tend to
the advancement of their weal.

Besides, the working year of the Protestants contained three
hundred and ten days; because they set aside only the fifty-two Sabbaths
and a few solemn holidays, which gave their industry the advantage of
one sixth over that of the Catholics, whose working year contained but
two hundred and sixty days, inasmuch as they set apart to rest above one
hundred and five days.

They adopted the system of combined labor. They organized their
establishments on the principle of the subdivision of labor, directed by
skilful directors, who employed thousands of workmen, whom they
stimulated by the lure of salaries duly proportioned to their services,
thus offering the surest and most ready method of arriving at the most
perfect, most abundant, and most economical production. As a result,
France possessed the finest manufactories of wool, and shared the rich
commerce in broadcloth which belonged to the English, the Hollander,
and the Italians.

The invention of the stocking loom increased the number of the
manufactories of stockings, of wool, silk, thread, and cotton. The
Protestants distinguished themselves in this new art, and propagated it in
the district of Sedan and Languedoc. A portion of that province, the
upper Gevaudon, a mountainous and sterile region, almost entirely
inhabited by the "Reformed" was celebrated for the serges and coddices
made. In that region all the peasants had trades. The children spun from
the age of four years and upward, and the whole of the family thus
found occupation.

It was the Protestants of France who gave the world the best linen
cloth. The tanneries of Touraine, the silk factories of Tours and Lyons,
were all owned and worked by Protestants.

Nor did the Protestants confine themelves to manufactures and commerce, but entered largely into all the liberal careers. Numbers of the Reformed distinguished themselves as physicians, as advocates, as writers, as well as preachers, and contributed largely to the glory of the age of Louis XIV. The eloquence of the pulpit at this date owed to the Protestants its extraordinary success; for while with Romanists preaching was but an accessory part of worship, it had become with their adversaries its most important feature.

"They ask only their bellyful of preaching," said Catherine de Medici, sneeringly, while she was yet vacillating between the two creeds. Having charge to teach the religion of the gospel, culture was essential, then as now. Hence, there shortly arose a rivalry between the two religions, from which the pulpits reaped good results. Because of the power of the pulpit, Bossuet, Massilon, Bourdalue and Fenelon became famed in the Catholic world as preachers more than priests. In all the principal cities of the kingdom, the Protestants maintained nourishing schools of learning. Grand as was this period in many respects, it was wanting in fidelity to the truth. When they knew the truth and had the opportunity, they failed to glorify it, neither were thankful.

The same men who had braved death and torture were found to be unarmed against Court favor. They had not the courage of their convictions. Expediency, rather than principle, ruled them.

In this land a similar state of things exists. Men are silent in regard to the aggressions of Rome, when a proclamation of the truth would overthrow error and cause errorists to flee. The surrender to Rome on the part of politicians was only matched by the conduct of the French when they might have spoken. The consequences of this betrayal can only be described in part.

An edict of the 17th of June, 1681, permitted hoys at fourteen, and girls at twelve, to abjure the Protestant religion, and re-enter the bosom of the Romish church.

This law was attended with terrible results. It undermined all parental authority in Protestant families. It is in line with the Romish claim that all sprinkled children are Romanists. It was enough that any one should affirm to the authorities that a child wished to become a Roman Catholic, having joined in prayer, or made the sign of the cross, or kissed the image of the Virgin, to cause his abstraction from the care of his parents, who were forced besides to pay him a pension; so that the loss of the child was followed by the loss of property.

The synods received an order to accept neither legacies nor donations. The ministers were forbidden to speak in their sermons of the wretchedness of the times, or to attack, directly or indirectly, the Roman Catholic religion. To all this the "Reformed" assented without remonstrance or resistance. They surrendered their liberties, and by so doing were destroyed.

After this, came the systematic attempt for the conversion of the Protestants. Troops were quartered upon them.

In many villages the priests followed the soldiers through the streets, crying, "Courage, gentlemen! it is the intention of the king that these dogs of Huguenots shall be pillaged and sacked."

The soldiers entered the houses, sword in hand, sometimes crying: "Kill, kill!" to frighten the women and the children. So long as the inhabitants could satisfy their rapacity, they suffered no more than pillage. But when their money was expended, the price of their furniture consumed, and the ornaments and garments of their wives disposed of, the dragoons seized them by the hair to drag them to church; or, if they suffered them to remain in their houses, made use of threats, outrages, and even tortures, to compel them to be converted. They burnt, at slow fires, the feet and hands of some; they broke the ribs, legs, or arms of others with blows of sticks. Others were cast into damp dungeons, with threats of leaving them there to rot. The soldiers said that everything was permitted to them except murder and rape.

On the 28th of July, 1681, Charles the Second was compelled to sanction a bill which granted the most extensive privileges to those French refugees who should demand an asylum in England. From Holland, and from Germany as well, a cry of indignation arose. Louis XIV. called a halt. The persecutions stopped for a time; but in 1684 they began again, and then it went from bad to worse.

New tortures were tried. Families were deprived of sleep by the noise of soldiers. The voice of drums, blasphemies, hideous cries, the crash of furniture, and constant shaking, by which they compelled these miserable wretches to stand up at night and keep their eyes open, were some of the means employed to deprive them of sleep. To pinch them, to prick them with sharp instruments, to pull them about, to suspend them with cords, and a hundred other cruelties, were the sport of these executioners, by which their hosts were reduced to such a state that they were glad to promise whatever they wished, to escape these barbarians. The soldiers offered indignities to women. They spat in their faces, they made them lie down on hot coals, and put their heads in heated ovens in which the vapor was enough to suffocate them.

As a result, thousands succumbed. It is a terrible picture, and the sufferings God's children were compelled to undergo are too horrid to relate.

Is there not a lesson for us? Can we not see the peril in surrendering to such a foe?

There was no pity in their hearts. They had no respect for citizenship. Bigotry ruled.

On the 22d of October, Louis XIV. signed at Fontainbleu, the revocation of the Edict of Nantes. The principal provisions of the revocation edict were the following: The Protestant temples were to be demolished, and the exercise of their religious worship was to cease, as well in private houses as in the castles of the nobles, on pain of confiscation of property and personal arrest. The ministers who should refuse to be converted, were warned to leave the kingdom within fourteen days, on pain of being sent to the galleys.

Protestant schools were to be closed; the children who were born after the publication of the edicts were to be baptized by the priests of their parishes and brought up in the Roman Catholic faith. A term of four months was granted to refugees wherein to return to France and apostatize; that time expired, their property was to be confiscated. Protestants were formally prohibited from leaving the kingdom and carrying their fortunes abroad, on pain of the galleys for men, and confiscation of their property and personal arrest for the women. All the provisions of the law against relapsed converts were confirmed.

The "Reformed" who had not changed their religion, were to remain in the kingdom until it should please God to enlighten them.

On the same day that the edict of revocation was registered, the destruction of the temple of Charentou, built by the celebrated architect Jacques Debrosse, and capable of containing 14,000 persons, was commenced. Five days afterward, no trace of the edifice remained. The church at Caen, which had so many times re-echoed to the eloquent voice of Dubas, fell in rums, to the flourish of trumpets and shouts of joy. At Nimes, Cheyrau was permitted to preach a last discourse. He did so, and appealed to his hearers to persevere in the faith unto death. The temple was torn down and became a heap of ruins. In the midst, could long be remarked a single stone, beneath the overthrown front, bearing this inscription:

"HERE IS THE HOUSE OF GOD, HERE IS THE GATE OF HEAVEN."

The Protestants who had believed Louis XIV. to be the greatest king of the age, and that he would yet see his mistake, had their eyes opened to the actual condition of affairs when they saw 800 temples destroyed, and learned that troops had been ordered into the North of France to complete the work done in the South.

Protestant servants were denied employment, and noblemen were compelled to employ Roman Catholics. These severities bore fruit. The galleys were filled with prisoners. Everybody that could escape, did so. To London, to Germany, to America, they came in uncounted numbers. France was emptied of its best population.

Over 1,300,000 of the good and well-to-do citizens went forth as exiles. In a celebrated memoir addressed to Louvais, in 1688, Voubon deplores the desertion of 1,000,000 men, the withdrawal of $60,000,000 of money, the ruin of commerce, the enemies' fleet increased by 9,000 of the best sailors of the kingdom, and their armies by 600 officers and 12,000 soldiers.

The north of France became depopulated, as well as the south. Of 1998 Protestant families who dwelt in the district of Paris, 1202 emigrated.

The priests celebrated the day of revocation by public thanksgiving. What sorrows followed in that train! A law passed by the constituent assembly of 1790, restored to the descendants, now dispersed over the face of the globe, the title of French citizens, on the simple condition of returning to France and fulfilling the civil duties imposed on all Frenchmen; but it could not bring back to France the loss which it had sustained. For almost a century the Roman Catholic church had full sway in the whole of France. It possessed all the edifices of worship, all the schools, the press, the government. The Protestants had lost the right of possessing their creed and the right of existing.

Treachery never pays, and wrong-doing secures terrible harvests. After St. Bartholomew came remorse to Charles IX. He lived but twenty-one months. He could not get away from the horrid memory. The man who had boasted on the fatal night that there should not be a single Huguenot left to reproach him with the deed, was waited on at his death-bed by a Huguenot nurse. "Alas, nurse, dear nurse," he would say to her, "what blood, what murders! Oh, my God! forgive me. What shall I do? I am lost." And the nurse would point him to God as the only hope.

Henry IV., after betraying his mother's and his soul's highest interests, was smitten by an assassin's dagger, and died as the fool dieth.

Louis XIV. saw his kingdom impoverished, his commerce gone, his name execrated throughout the world, and lay in his magnificent palace at Versailes dying. He is utterly wretched. The people curse him, and hurl stones and mud at his coffin.

The church of Rome gains nothing but infamy. The Revolution struck with awful justice and rent the fetters of French Protestantism, smiting into the dust the throne which had so long oppressed them.

And so Protestantism is revived. There about 1,000,000 Protestants. Many of them have acquired a distinguished place in the Church and in the State.

1. France lost the light, because Christians hid it beneath a bushel. They forgot that they were the light, and if they refused to let their light shine they increased the gloom. They enjoyed the truth; but they did not preach it. The aggressive gospel of Luther and Zwingle was set aside. They turned to money-getting and thrift, and left the affairs of State to others.

John Knox, with his words, spoken and written, drove his enemies into their retreats. By his addresses and sermons he made public opinion, roused the popular heart, and directed the popular will. In France there was no such man. There was too little enlightened opinion. The military spirit died with the moral. It was not the call to arms, no more than the call to repentance. It was not the fight for liberty, because it was not the good fight of faith.

2. *Their second great mistake was in proclaiming the possibility of a Romanist being saved while he clings to the errors of Rome.*

For this the leaders argued, even as men argue it now. In our churches are ministers and men who claim that the Roman Catholic church stands in association with evangelical churches as a church of Christ. In the discussion of the Freedom of Worship Bill, this position was maintained.

Romanists are treated not as errorists; but as if, despite their errors, they are Christians. In faith and practice they are Pagans. We are not speaking against them as citizens, but denying that they are Christians, while they are Romanists. They are in peril because tradition is preferred to Scripture, Mary to Jesus, and the decrees of the church to the commands of Christ. They must have the Gospel brought to them, and they must believe it to the saving of their souls, or they must be lost.

"Venerable ministers of the Gospel," exclaimed Rev. Charles Chiniquy, "Rome is the great danger ahead for the church of Christ, and you do not understand it enough. The atmosphere of light, honesty, truth, and holiness in which you are born, and which you have breathed since your infancy, makes it almost impossible for you to realize the dark mysteries of idolatry, immorality, degrading slavery, hatred of the Word of God, concealed behind the walls of that modern Babylon. It is that ignorance which paves the way for the triumph of Rome. It paralyzes the arm of the church of Christ."

WHY THIS INDIFFERENCE?

The answer of this man, who was fifty years a priest, is: "Because modern Prostestants have not only forgotten what Rome was, what she is, and what she will forever be, the most irreconcilable and powerful enemy of the gospel of Christ; but while she is striking Christians to the heart, by cursing their schools and wrenching the Bible from the hands of the children ; while she is battering down and scaling the walls and storming the citadel of their faith, they are recognizing her as a branch of the church of Christ.

IT IS A DELUSION AND A SNARE.

Rome, that shed the blood of our forefathers, that refused to keep faith with heretics, that fired the inquisition, and lit its fires with devilish and malignant joy, is in our midst, attempting to chain our people to the feet of her idols.

Romanists, that murdered Henry IV., that stabbed Coligni to the heart, that burned a Huss, a Ridley and a Latimer, and that plotted the death of Abraham Lincoln, and attempted to stab Liberty, are here to fight with desperation, and do their utmost to destroy the liberty our fathers fought for, and we have defended.

ROME NEVER COMPROMISES.

Upon the ministry of this hour, a fearful responsibility is devolved. Let them reckon Roman Catholics as a part of the religious world, who can be saved while they adhere to the errors of Rome, and the people will see no cause for alarm, and no reason why efforts should be made to rescue the millions in our midst from the grasp of the destroyer.

Let them proclaim the truth, that Rome hates the Bible, destroys the Sabbath, apologizes for crime, and teaches that a criminal coming to the confessional may, by the act of a priest, become white as a saint, and the people will see a reason for jails and penitentiaries being filled with members in good standing of the Roman Catholic church. They will see that honesty and integrity are imperilled by such teaching. Romanism is a lie, coined in hell, and built up as a system through the machinations of Satan. It must be resisted, and Romanists must be warned of their peril, because they who believe in such error are damned. It is our duty to preach the gospel to our prisoners. This may be their only opportunity to hear the truth. Romanism cannot usurp the place of Christianity without destroying the foundations of liberty. The Christians of this land must fearlessly proclaim the truth, if they will save the State.

It was the boast of Napoleon that he made way for the talents. But such talents! Talents wriggling to a height where the lion could scarcely find a foothold, or the eagle a place to perch!

It was, and is, the Bible that opens the way for the talents. Because of this redemption has come, and where it is welcomed, and loved and used, there is prosperity. Life tells. God takes care of his own.

A third mistake was made when they consented, for any reason, to be silent concerning the errors of Rome.

This peril confronts us. Pulpits are closed against this. Professors of religion apologize for, if they do not champion, the errors of Rome. While the Huguenot consented to be silent, Rome worked on. The result was seen not only in the Revocation of the Edict of Nantes, but in the state of affairs which made that revocation a possibility.

It is not safe to forget the drift and trend of Romanism. All who keep their eye on public affairs, know that Romanism is organizing for the battle of Armageddon. The *Watchman of* St. Louis boldly says: "There are indications that before the next half century has passed, the two great bodies into which Christianity is divided will engage in a real conflict, in which the strength of the seminal principle of each communion will be put to a real test."

"Finally, my brethren, be strong in the Lord, and in the power of his might. Put on the whole armor of God, that ye may be able to stand against the wiles of the devil." Some one must fight, if truth shall reign. Americans have great trusts committed to their keeping.

The need of the hour is an awakened church. Luther could not have got on without the Elector of Saxony. John Wicliff would have been a failure had not the Duke of Lancaster stood by and for him. Pray that some of our mighty laymen, now giving money for colleges and churches, may lay their offerings on this altar, and help us to sow the broad fields of our American life with Gospel seed.

At the battle of Gettysburg, one hundred and fifty cannons poured their leaden and iron hail upon our men. It seemed difficult to live in the galling fire. Our soldiers were burrowing in the ground, hiding behind what they could place before them, when they heard a band of music. At its head rode Hancock, hat off, saying to the men: "Gentlemen, that cannonade means that our enemies are getting ready to attack us. Be ready. Prove to be men." Our boys were ready; and when the battle-wave struck the Rock of Patriotism, it broke, and victory came,—in which the South glories now equally with the North.

So shall it be in this fight with Rome. The defeat of Rome is the salvation of the Republic, and the deliverance of Romanists from superstition, that produces the sleep of death. Let us glorify God as God, and work while it is day.

15

Romish Schools Our Peril

ROME IS AN OLD FIGHTER. In the battle now raging for the utter overthrow of the public school system in the United States, Rome is managing her forces and planting her blows in accordance with well-defined plans; which, having won victories elsewhere, she believes are sure to produce the same results in her present desperate encounter. Thousands in pulpits and in pews, in shops and on farms, think resistance worse than folly. This class are either betraying the youth of America, or are silent while others are doing the infamous work. It is time to call a halt. For more than fifty years, because of this false security which has held the church in the arms of a delusive slumber, and through the cowardice or ambition of party leaders, this nation, with all its unparalleled opportunities and responsibilities has been drifting toward a surrender of the children to the control of the priests of Rome. Rome's opposition is open and defiant. It has assumed four distinct phases:

1. In 1840, Archbishop Hughes gave this order: "Take the children out of the public schools, as you would take them out of devouring fire;" that was to get them away from Bible influence. First, denounce the schools because the Bible is read; then banish the Bible and denounce them as godless—is the programme of Rome.

2. The Bible having been removed as a text-book, Rome fought general education, and became the open and avowed champion of illiteracy.

3. In 1884, the Plenary Council ordered the building of parochial schools. The decree was mandatory; save in cases where a sufficient cause can be shown, satisfactory to the bishop. Neglect of this requirement subjected the offender to the usual penalties of disobedience. This was the beginning of the trouble with Edward

McGlynn. Educated in the public schools, he believes in them and fought for them.

4. The children of Roman Catholics have been taken out of the schools, and now they claim the right of giving direction as to how the children of Protestants shall be educated. The inquiry has been raised, If the schools are so bad that Roman Catholic children cannot attend them, are they not too bad for Roman Catholic teachers to teach in them? If Romanists insist on educating their children, ought they not to stop all interference on their part with the educating of children not belonging to them?

Vicar-General Brady, of St. Louis, declares: "We are doing all that we can to prevent our children from going to the public schools. We must educate our own children. They are educated in the public schools merely as animals would be educated. Their souls are not attended to."

In Monseigneur Segur's "Plain Talk About Protestantism," there is this language (p. 98): "The freedom of thinking is simply nonsense. We are no more free to think without rule, than we are to act without one." Page 105: "We have to believe only what the Pope and the Bishops teach. We have to reject only that which the Pope and the Bishops condemn and reject. Should a point of doctrine appear doubtful, we have only to address ourselves to the Pope and the Bishops to know what to believe. Only from that tribunal, forever living and forever guided by God, emanate true judgment on religious belief, and particularly on the true sense of Scripture."

The Roman Church, claiming to understand the secrets of God and to have the keys of heaven and hell, and blasphemously presuming that it can control the destinies of men—to save eternally or damn forever in a life to come—undertakes to bestow for money the joys of the former, and inflict the pains of the latter, on those who refuse credulity and cash. To make this trade prosperous, ignorance is a necessity. "It uses money, mendacity and pretended miracles, to capture and enslave the ignorant. It assails everything tending to enlighten the masses, on whose ignorance it feeds. Italy, Spain, Ireland, Mexico and Lower Canada sufficiently illustrate its terrible work. Human vitality and intelligence have probably been brought to a lower point in Spain than in any other civilized nation on the globe, and the Roman Church is largely, if not solely, responsible for this national degradation and ruin. It seeks to do—is most successfully preparing to do—is doing slowly—for the United States what it has done for Spain. Our free-school system destroyed, political integrity destroyed and parties corrupted, the goal is not far away."

2.. THE CHARACTER OF THE EDUCATION GIVEN DESERVES NOTICE.

The trouble in Ireland to-day is, that England is dealing with a people who believe that all is right which is done to advance the power of the Church. Hence, there, as here, jurymen utterly ignore the value of their oath where the interests of the Church require it. For this reason alone, the right of "trial by jury" is threatened.

ROMANISM GIVES A LICENSE TO VIOLATE,

in some way or other, every precept of the Decalogue. If men who are Romanists are truthful, honest and upright, it is because they are better than the religion they profess compels them to be.

Rome teaches that the Sabbath may be set aside after hearing mass. Merchandizing and the selling of goods at auction is permitted on the Sabbath. He who performs any servile work on the Lord's Day or on a festival day, let him do penance three days on bread and water. If any one breaks fasts prescribed by the Church, let him do penance on bread and water twenty days. Three days on bread and water for disobeying their God; twenty days for disobeying their Church! Absolution is given for stealing small amounts to pay for masses, though the law is, that masses shall be given without pay. The command: "Thou shalt have no other gods before me," is blotted out of the Bible by papal hands. Children trained in these schools can lie, steal, break the Sabbath, and commit sins of any kind, and obtain absolution from a man no better than the guilty party.

The oath of allegiance, by which the thousands of Romanists have obtained the rights of the ballot, citizenship and office, which, if regarded as obligatory, would bind every one of them to support the principles of Republican Government, is valueless; because, whenever Roman officials shall see fit to require this oath to be disregarded, every good Romanist, to a man, is bound by his allegiance to the Pope, which he believes more binding than his allegiance to the Government, to disregard it. As proof, we quote from "Abridged Course of Religious Instruction for the Use of Colleges and Schools," by the Rev. Father F. X. Schouppe, of the Society of Jesus, with the imprimateur of H. E. Cardinal Manning, London—Burns and Gates, 1880, p. 203: "The Church can dispense from a promissory oath. This power belongs to the Pope and bishops, who exercise it either themselves or by their delegates."

Page 278: "The civil laws (of Christendom) are binding in conscience so long as they are conformable to the rights of the Catholic Church."

This gives a warrant to the false swearing which floods our cities with voters who have passed from their landing in this free country to the courts where they take a false oath, to the polls, where, with another false oath, they swear in their vote, and to the confessional, where their oath is held to be a justifiable, "dispensable" lie for the benefit of the Holy Roman Catholic Church, whenever it shall chance so to regard it, or order him so to regard it. He also is taught, "that the Sacrifice of the Mass remits sins and the punishment due them" (p. 210). "The power to remit sin is judicial. The priests are made judges of the sin and the disposition of the sinner. Their absolution is just as efficacious as would be that of Jesus Christ."

Educate the youth in this way, and "repeating" at the polls becomes an act of grace, and honest elections become an impossibility. As has been said: "A ship-load of foreign Romanists lands in New York; indulgence in the lump is by the Cardinal or Archbishop granted, to swear that they have resided here long enough to become citizens; they go before the court, become naturalized, get their final papers, and at once go to the polls and help elect the Cardinal's candidate for Mayor. Thus perjured citizens capture polling places and carry elections in the interest of Romanism."* It does not stop here.

Dissimulation is lawful, according to Liguori, as is gambling. "Laymen, or even the clergy, do not sin if they play cards principally for the sake of recreation, or for a moderate sum of money. Hence, gambling among priests is extensively practised.

DRUNKENNESS NOT A VICE.

"It is lawful to administer the sacraments to drunkards, if they are in danger of death, and had previously expressed a desire of receiving them." Hence, the murderer executed in the Tombs October 18th, 1883, cried for whiskey at the last, though he had partaken of the Eucharist. Priests are known to drink to excess. One, in a country town, rode home drunk almost every Sabbath evening after performing vespers in the chapel. All knew it, and it was tolerated because the guilty debauchee was a priest. It was Liguori who said: "Among the priests who live in the world, it is rare, very rare, to find one that is good."

Alexander Campbell, in his discussion with Archbishop Purcell, read from Liguori the permission for priests to keep nieces, or concubines. Archbishop Purcell denied that Liguori ever taught anything so abominable, and that all who say so are guilty of a flagrant violation of the commandment which says, "Thou shalt not bear false witness against thy neighbor." The book was brought in, and another read therefrom these words: "A bishop, however poor he may be, cannot appropriate to himself pecuniary fines without the license of the Apostolical See; but he ought to apply to pious uses that which the Council of Trent has laid upon non-resident clergymen, or upon those clergymen who keep concubines." Marriage is a mortal sin. Adultery is pardoned.

---

* Romanism, by A. J. Grover, p. 18.

"What answer ought a confessor to give when questioned concerning a truth which he knows from sacramental confession only?"

"He ought to answer that he does not know it, and, if it be necessary, to confirm the same with an oath."

"Is it lawful, then, to tell a lie?"

"He is questioned as a man, and answers as a man. As a man he does not know the truth, though he knows it as God."

"What if a confessor were directly asked whether he knows it through sacramental confession?"

"He may reply, "I know nothing.""

Is such a religion good enough for the youth of America? It is the true position that the nation has no right to give children into the hands of Roman Catholics; and that prisoners in our penal institutions ought to be taught and helped by men who believe and teach the Word of God?

ROMAN CATHOLICS SHOULD NOT HAVE CHARGE OF PRISONS.

Jerry McCauley, the river thief, and a most desperate character, went to *Sing Sing* as a member of the Roman Catholic communion, in full and in good standing, as are the majority of our prisoners in all our penal institutions. It was because Jerry McCauley heard the Gospel and found a Bible in his room that he was converted, came out of the Church of Rome, and became a benefactor to hundreds of thousands.

3. THE STATE HAS NO RIGHT TO RECOGNIZE THE CHURCH.

If the Court of Special Sessions can commit to a Roman Catholic institution children between seven and fourteen years of age, as idle, truant, vicious, or homeless, then the State can put its neck into the yoke Rome has been framing for many years, with the consent of a silent Christianity and a crafty political sentiment. The law says,

The free exercise and enjoyment of religious profession and worship, without discrimination or preference, shall forever be allowed in this State for all mankind.

The Constitution of these United States, in providing for religious liberty, expressly declares that no restraint should be exercised: "that Congress should make no law respecting an establishment of religion, or prohibiting the free exercise thereof;" but recognizing the principle introduced to the notice of mankind by Roger Williams, who repudiated toleration, because the right to tolerate implied the right to persecute; who would not accept as a favor from man what had been given to him as a right by God; who held that, when God made the eye he conferred the right to look, and when he made the Bible he conferred the right to read it, or have it read.

Gambetta, in France, saw this peril, and warned the State against giving over children to the control of priests to be educated and guided by them. "I am," said the great French statesman, "for the separation of the schools from the churches. I consider this not only a question of political, but of social order. Let not Catholics, with their claims to exclusiveness, have anything to do with the propagation of necessary knowledge, which it is the State's duty to see imparted to every citizen."

Gambetta knew Romanism as we in this free land do not know it. Let us hear, and heed his manly advice.

The parochial school, notwithstanding the disposition of the American people to try and conciliate their Roman Catholic fellow-citizens, is a fact. The decree has gone forth from the Provincial Council, sanctioned by the Pope, that such schools shall be built in every parish. Compromise is a failure. Not only does Rome seek to take her children out of our public schools; but, under one pretence or another, she seeks to fill these public schools with Roman Catholic teachers. Let us have done with this. Put the Bible back where it belongs. Let it become a text-book for the children of America. Teach them to be good readers of the Scriptures. Said Sir William Jones, who was familiar with Greek, Roman and Oriental literature: "The Bible, independently of its

Divine origin, contains more sublimity, purer morality, more impartial history and finer strains of eloquence than can be collected from any other book, in whatever language it may have been written." John Jay, in an admirable address on "Rome, the Bible and the Republic," quotes the distinguished Robert Hall as saying: "Wherever the Scriptures are generally read, the standard of morals is raised," and adds: "The indebtedness of this country to the Bible, and its recognition by our Government in other days, are things not to be forgotten; and it is well to keep permanently before our people this distinguishing feature of our history." The great body of the original settlers on our newly discovered continent were men whose ancestors had fought for civil and religious freedom on the various battle-fields of the old world. They loved liberty, and loved God's Word. Is it not true that their love of liberty sprung from the influence of the truth upon their hearts? Follow the Bible around the world, and in its trail you find liberty, progress and enlightenment. The Bible ought to be made a textbook in every institution helped by the State, because of what the Bible does for the State. "There never was found," said Lord Bacon, "in any age of the world, either religion or law that did so highly exalt the public good as the Bible." If Romanists do not like it, let them dislike it. What they love, hurts liberty. What they hate, helps it. It is our duty to make our schools so good that no ambitious child of the State can afford to be educated elsewhere. I make my appeal to you, not as religionists, but as citizens,—Do more than refuse to divide the School Fund. Do this: from this time on, provide for children between seven and fourteen years of age who may be idle, truant, vicious or homeless, better places in which to educate them than the protectories or convents under Romish control. They are children of the State. Give them religious instruction, by giving them access to the Word of God. It is our bounden duty to teach them Christian morality, essential to their education as good citizens. In the words of Ulysses S. Grant:

"Let us labor to add all needful guarantees for the most perfect security of free thought, free speech, and free press, pure morals, unfettered religious sentiments, and of equal rights and privileges to all men, irrespective of nationality, color or religion. Encourage free schools, and resolve that not 'one dollar in money, no matter how raised, shall be appropriated to the support of any sectarian school.' Resolve that either the State, or nation, or both combined, shall support institutions of learning, sufficient to afford every child growing up in the land the opportunity of a good common school education."

POPERY IN THE UNITED STATES

is little known. It is hidden. It works in darkness. Such is the courage and faith of the American people that they consent to the existence of Roman Catholics, and to carry out their purposes and plans as they do the existence of Methodists or Baptists, or any religious denomination. They act as if it were ungenerous and unfair to uncover the wiles of Jesuitism, and disclose the perils which threaten the nation because of the doings of Romanism. In Canada, the actions of this desperate foe can be studied in detail. The programme with which the people of the United States is confronted has been carried out. There, Rome is dominant. The harvest of Rome has ripened, and Rome is consolidated.

SEPARATE OR PAROCHIAL SCHOOLS EXIST IN CANADA

under the sanction of the law. They are sustained by taxation, as are Protestant schools; and there are many ways in which Roman Catholics are permitted to place Protestants at a disadvantage:

1. Five Roman Catholics can petition for a separate school. The petition being granted, all Roman Catholics within a radius of three miles every way can be compelled to support it. No matter if they prefer the public school, the law compels them to support the Roman Catholic school. All known to be Roman Catholics, and all believed to be Roman Catholics, are taxed, and deliverance from the same can only be obtained by a process of law, which is irritating, if not dangerous.

2. All Protestant teachers are compelled to go through a public examination, and must measure up to a certain grade, or fail in obtaining a school. In Roman Catholic schools, the Christian Brothers and Nuns

can be appointed without examination. Today, the teachers of parochial schools are not examined in the United States, and the schools are not inspected; the youth are surrendered to Rome.

3. For the Protestant schools, books are selected by the Board of Public Education. In Roman Catholic schools, they select their own, and may fill them with treason, with superstition and paganism, and there is none to say them Nay.

4. In the public schools the Bible is read; not in Roman Catholic schools.

5. The public schools are inspected; not the Roman Catholic.

6. In the election of trustees for public schools, a secret ballot is used. In Roman Catholic school districts, the trustees are elected by their signing their names, and voting Aye or Nay. This is the fight now going on. The laity want the secret ballot, that they may get rid of priestly control. The open ballot is kept, to preserve the control of the priests.

As a result, Roman Catholic children are growing up in ignorance. It is proven in Canada, as in Ireland, or Spain, or Mexico, that Rome hates education.

Doctor Maguire, a Roman Catholic professor of the University of Dublin, and one of the senators of the Royal University of Ireland, has written a pamphlet on

THE EFFECTS OF HOME RULE ON EDUCATION,

in which he declares "that a large and logical section of the Roman Catholic Church is conscientiously opposed to the spread of education." He quotes the *Dublin Review* (vol. xx., p. 192, second series), in which it is contended, "that the absence of higher education is a powerful preservative against apostacy," and tells a story of the Archbishop of Tuam, who closed a school, and when one of the villagers asked how he was to send his children to school, replied: *"What do they want with a school? Let them learn their Catechism."*

Cardinal Cullen, in 1870, before the Educational Convention, said: "It is admitted that the Scotch and the Irish are of the same origin, and shows that since the Scotch embraced the Reformed religion they have

183

outrun even the English; while, wherever the Irish embraced Romanism, they have retrograded." What a contrast between exclusively Roman Catholic Connaught and Protestant Ulster!

Education is the basis of national liberty and prosperity. In elementary instruction, Protestant States are incomparably more advanced than Roman Catholic, and representative governments are the natural outgrowth of Protestant populations; while despotic governments are the congenial governments of Roman Catholic populations.

DeLavelieye declares, that "the control of education by the Roman priesthood leads inevitably to illiteracy, with its tendency to degradation, pauperism and crime."

The *Roman Catholic Review* for April, 1871, said: "We do not indeed prize as highly as some of our countrymen appear to do, the ability to read, write and cipher. *Some men are born to be leaders, and the rest are born to be led.* The best ordered and administered State is that in which the few are well educated and lead, and the many trained to obedience."

Said a priest: "I would as soon administer the sacraments to a dog, as to a Catholic who sent his children to a public school."

THIS IS ROMANISM.

It ought to be fought; not for the sake of Protestants alone, but because of the imperilled interests of the children of Roman Catholics. Illiteracy imperils, here and everywhere.

In Canada, one-sixth of the population furnishes more than five-sixths of the crime. Occasional disclosures reveal this peril. When the bill was introduced into the Legislature of New York, pretending to secure freedom of worship, it was proven to have been proposed by a Jesuit, and was introduced by Senator Gibbs; "because," as he said in a letter to the New York *Evening Post,* Oct. 27, 1875, "of certain pledges made by the leading Republicans to the Irish Catholic voters for their support of James G. Elaine." If in America, with our centuries of training in the principles of Republican government, with our hereditary devotion to the elementary principles of civil and religious freedom, such bargains can be made, and Irish votes can be sold in blocks for the betrayal of the principles of the Constitution, is is not time to ask if Popery be not in the way?

The American people are generous to a fault. They have treated Romanists as if they were brothers. They have been slow to believe they were tolerating an enemy. They are waking up. They are seeing the peril threatening liberty. They are getting on their armor, and they will fight the good fight of faith; and, though a little slow in starting, they will get there all the same; and will yet have the honor of digging as deep a grave for Romanism as they have furnished for human slavery. They are becoming weary of such sentiments as, that "Too much education would make the poor discontented with their lot, and unsuit them for following the plow, using the spade, hammering iron, or building walls." It is American to believe in education for the people; and to thank God that the path opens to the highest positions from the door of a hovel as well as from the door of a palace. In our public schools, the rich and poor are equals. As Macaulay said:

"During the last three centuries, to stunt the growth of the human mind has been her chief object. Throughout Christendom, whatever advance has been made in knowledge, in freedom, in wealth, and in the arts of life, has been in inverse proportion to her power. The loveliest and most fertile provinces of Europe have, under her rule, been sunk in poverty, in political servitude, and in intellectual torpor; while Protestant countries, once proverbial for sterility and barbarism, have been turned by skill and industry into gardens, and can boast of a long list of heroes, statesmen, philosophers and poets."

WHAT IS NEXT?

Rome will soon have her children housed in the parochial school buildings. Then will come the refusal to pay taxes. Property will be levied and held up for sale. Who will buy it? They who do so, will run the peril of losing their lives. The scenes of Ireland will be re-enacted in the United States. Then will come the end. The American people will make short work of Romanism, when once they understand its motives, its animus and purpose.

THE REMEDY.

Resist this devil of Romanism and it will flee. Put the Bible back where it belongs; and make it a reading-book for the youth of America. Adopt the Prussian system, or devise a better, and see to it that the children of the State are given religious instruction; so that they shall know the chief doctrines of the Bible, the life and teachings of our Lord, the history of the Christian religion in connection with contemporary civil history. Let there be no sectarianism taught, and no antagonism engendered, and then shall our schools become the bulwark and defence of liberty.

16

Parochial Schools and Indulgences

THE MORNING COMETH; AND with it, and before it, the struggle. In Pennsylvania, and notably in Pittsburg, Romanism is doing its worst. Bless God for a McCrory, a Riddle, and many more brave and eloquent men, who have sounded out the bugle-call to action. There they seek to take possession of the public school buildings for parochial school purposes. The language of Superintendent Higbee furnishes good reading. He says:

"In the case submitted to us, it is stated that the Board of Directors have rented or leased a public school building for the use of a parochial school, where the peculiar dogmas and usages of a particular church, or where only a certain distinct class of children, are admitted. In this case, granting the statement of facts, there is not only an unauthorized violation of trust, but a seeming indifference to what is explicitly forbidden by the constitution of the Commonwealth itself. A school is not sectarian because taught by a minister, or priest, or any church official; but a school controlled or managed in the interest of any particular church organization, upholding its peculiar confession and ecclesiastical practices, and used for any class of pupils exclusive of others, is certainly sectarian. It does not in any sense belong to our system of public schools; on the contrary, no money raised for the support of the public schools can be used for its support without a direct violation of the constitution. Were school directors permitted to lease our public property thus, at their own will, for the use of parochial schools, the ecclesiastical convictions of the directors could turn our public schools into as many different kinds of church schools as there are different denominations in the Commonwealth."

If the opinion of the State Superintendent of schools should fail to induce the offending school board to abandon their position, the case will be appealed to the courts.

The home is being stirred. In New York, the imperilled condition of the little ones is coming to the surface. It is found that in New York and Brooklyn, and many of our large cities, Romanists find it convenient to have the children shut out of school privileges. In New York, after counting noses, it is found that there are 20,000 children of school-age in this city for whom no room is provided in the school buildings. These little ones are of the class who most need to be provided for, being the children of poor people, who cannot afford them private instruction, and whose education must necessarily be completed by the time they are fourteen years old. None of the grammar schools are crowded, but in all the primary schools the pupils are huddled together like sheep, and are left always to the care of the least experienced teachers.

The City says, it cannot afford to build schoolhouses enough to supply the demand, or at least its Board of Education says so. Yet it maintains a free college, with a big faculty, where only twenty out of every class remain to graduate, and pays for a normal school which has 2,000 girl pupils, only one-seventh of whom remain for the four years of the course. These two institutions are the special pets of the Board, and everything else is sacrificed to them. If any of the English nobility are in the town they are taken up to the normal school to see 1,000 bright-faced American girls go through their calisthenic exercises, and are gravely told that this is a specimen of our educational system. They are never taken to the primary schools.

In Boston, another line of attack is being made by the church of Rome. "Swinton's Outlines of History "has been removed from the Boston schools on the vote of the majority of the School Committee, of whom 13 are Protestants and 11 liberal Roman Catholics. The passage which caused the exclusion of the work is the one relating to the institution of the sale of indulgences. This is the beginning of another grand assault, in a different direction, upon our American free school system. First, it was the Bible that Papists couldn't tolerate, and miserably weak-kneed, compromising Protestants all over the land were willing to expel the Bible from the schools in order to placate the

Papists. But it was soon discovered that it was not the Bible, but the schools, which Roman prelates and priests disliked so much.

Now these men, who cannot tolerate our public school system, begin to find fault with the text-books, claiming that our books on history do not teach what is true. They say, the facts of history concerning the Roman hierarchy are falsified, and the best way to remedy the matter is to bundle the books right out of the schools!

The Evangelical Alliance uttered their protest. Brice S. Evans, and other patriotic citizens, called a meeting in Faneuil Hall, and uttered their protest, asking that the Swinton's book be put back. This is their reply:

"The Board has been asked by a petition from members of the Evangelical Alliance, to reverse its decision and restore the book to the list. By reference, this request has been considered by the Committee, and a hearing has been given to the representatives of the Evangelical Alliance. In the judgment of the Committee, no reasons have been presented which should determine the Board to change its action.

The reasons assigned are as follows:

"1. The book . . . has in its favor ten years of public endorsement and use. It has had a long and honorable tenure of our public schools."

To retain books in the schools on this ground, would be to resist all improvement in the quality of text-books, and deprive the pupils of the benefit of progress in the provision of new matter, and better forms of instruction.

"2. The paragraph and footnote, on account of which the book has been rejected, contain a true statement of history."

They do not contain an ample and definite statement of the topic concerning which complaint has been justly made, to the effect that it was incorrectly taught.

"3. The book ejected is upon the expurgatory list of books of a certain religious sect."

The Committee were not aware of this fact; it did not enter into the grounds or affect the motives of their action.

Quoted from "Instructions to Catholics," by Rev. Xavier Donald Macleod. Boston: Murphy McCarthy.

"By an indulgence is meant the remission of the temporal punishment due to sins already forgiven. Every sin, however grievous, is remitted through the sacrament of penance, or by an act of perfect contrition, as regards its guilt and the eternal punishment due to it. But the debt of temporal punishment is not always remitted at the same time. The latter is done away with by deep penitence, or by works of satisfaction, e.g., prayers, alms, fasting, etc., or by patient endurance of troubles and adversities sent us by God, or by the satisfaction of our Lord Jesus Christ and the saints, applied to us by the church under certain conditions, which application we call an indulgence.

"An indulgence, then, is not a pardon for sin; because sin must be remitted before an indulgence can be gained. Much less is it a permission to commit sin, . . . for even God himself could not give such permission.

"In order to gain any indulgence whatever, you must be in a state of grace."

But it is added: "For this Committee of free citizens to put its expurgatorial stamp upon the book for the reasons alleged, is for it to ally itself with that religious sect."

In the judgment of your Committee, the course of action they have recommended was in the direct line of their steadfast purpose not to ally themselves either with or against any religious sect whatever. The Committee, therefore, recommend the following:

The School Committee have given careful consideration to your petition and to the reasons presented by your representatives as to the grounds on which it is based, and respectfully reply to the same: That they are not able to grant the request. They have found no cause to change their judgment, that the action taken with respect to the "Outlines of the World's History," in view of their whole responsibility and all the interests committed to their charge, and all the circumstances, was just.

JOHN G. BLAKE,
JOSEPH T. DURYEA,
JOSEPH D. FALLON.

Fortunate is it for the American people that this fight has been begun in Boston. Public attention had been called to the aggressions of Romanism. In "Why Priests Should Wed" (p 303), attention was directed to a sermon preached by Rev. Joseph T. Duryea, D. D., in the pulpit of the First Baptist church, on Thanksgiving Day, 1887, in which he sought to remove all apprehension or alarm because of the attack made by the Roman Catholic church upon our public school system. He said: "I have no religious prejudices." He further says: "I recognize the beneficent service to humanity of the Roman Catholic church during the dark ages." Then and there it was shown, that Rome made the ages "dark" by extinguishing every light in her power, and by putting to death millions of the lovers of Christ. The bid for the support of the Roman Catholic church was a success. At a public meeting, in which the pastor of the Congregational church met with Roman Catholics as friends and brothers, he told them of his having bowed down to the Pope of Rome and of having received his blessing. Whether he surrendered to the church, and took the vows of a Jesuit, and continues in the service of the Congregational church that he may do the more harm to Protestantism and more service to Romanism, is not known by the American people. Jesuitism provides for, and pays well for such service as the Rev. Joseph T. Duryea, D. D., is now rendering. The Protestants of New England owe it to the future of their youth that his influence be withstood, and his servility to error exposed.

The following petition was drawn up and has been largely signed and sent to this recreant minister:

"WHEREAS, The Rev. Joseph T. Duryea, D. D., lacks either the intelligence necessary to formulate a correct opinion concerning indulgences as taught by popes and practised by priests, or the honesty and bravery to tell the truth, preferring to ally himself with the Roman Catholic Church, the open and avowed enemy of public education, and the declared champion of illiteracy here and throughout the world: We, therefore, whose names are set to this petition, for the sake of imperilled youth, most respectfully ask him to resign his position on the School Board, and give place to a better educated, or a more truth loving man."

Let us turn attention to the statement authorized by the Committee in regard to indulgences, and confute it. They say: "By an indulgence is meant, the remission of the temporal punishment due to sins already forgiven." That is as far from being truth as Romanists, helped by a Congregational minister, can make it. Indulgences were an invention of Urban II. in the eleventh century, as a recompense for those who went in person upon the enterprise of conquering the Holy Land. They were afterwards granted to those who hired a soldier for that purpose; and in process of time were bestowed on such as gave money for accomplishing any pious work enjoined by the Pope. The dogma is as follows:

"That all good works of the saints, over and above those which were necessary toward their own justification, are deposited, together with the infinite merits of Jesus Christ, in one inexhaustible treasury. The keys of this were committed to St. Peter, and to his successors, the popes, who may open it at pleasure, and by transferring a portion of this superabundant merit to any particular person, for a sum of money, may convey to him either the pardon of his own sins, or a release for any one in whom he is interested from the pains of purgatory."

This is through and through an utter rejection of Christ, in whom our life is hid; and because we put off anger, wrath, malice, blasphemy, filthy communication, and put on the new man, permitting the word of Christ to dwell in us richly, the Christian looks upon his own righteousness as filthy rags. Christ is all and in all.

LOOK AT TETZEL.

He enters towns in procession, companies of priests bearing candles and banners, choristers chanting and ringing bells. At the churches a red cross was set upon the altars, a silk banner floating from it with the papal arms, and a great iron dish at the foot to receive the equivalents for the myriads of years in the penal fire of Tartarus. He came to Wittenberg. Luther's flock bought indulgences. It was cheaper than going to confession. Luther was compelled to pronounce against them, pope or no pope. This he did; and declared that no man's sins could be pardoned by them.

IT WAS THE BEGINNING OF THE REFORMATION.

On it went, deepening and widening like a mighty river, sweeping all before it. Then, to the door of the church he nailed the theses against indulgences, on the last day of October, 1517.

There were ninety-five of them. Tetzel replied, or got some one to reply for him, and burned Luther's books. The students of Wittenberg stood by Luther and made a bonfire of 800 books of Tetzel. The act showed their contempt for indulgences. The pope stood for the lie, and against the brave man telling the truth, and issued a bull against the monk. The Pope always stands for a lie. His feet are planted on a lie. If there were no lie there would be no Pope.

The purgatorial theory is built on a lie. Indulgences are linked with it.

THE FORM OF INDULGENCES THEN GIVEN

was as follows: " May our Lord Jesus Christ have mercy upon thee, and absolve thee by the merits of his most holy passion. And by his authority, and of his blessed apostles Peter and Paul, and of the most holy pope, granted and committed to me in these parts, do absolve thee, first, from all ecclesiastical censures, in whatever form they have been incurred; then, from all thy sins, transgressions, excesses, how enormous so ever they may be, even from such as are reserved for the cognizance of the Holy See, and as far as the keys of the holy church extend. I remit to you all punishment which you deserve in purgatory on that account; and I restore you to the holy sacraments of the church, to the unity of the faithful, and to that innocence and purity which you possessed at baptism; so that when you die the gates of punishment shall be shut, and the gates of the paradise of delights shall be opened; and if you shall not die at present, this grace shall remain in full force when you are at the point of death." Can any delusion be worse?

The statements made by the Romanists, with the assent of the Congregational minister, is, that indulgences remit the temporal punishment of sins forgiven—to this they add: "Every sin, however grievous, is remitted through the sacrament of penance, or by an act of perfect contrition, as regards its guilt and the eternal punishment due to it. But the debt of temporal punishment is not always remitted at the same time. The latter is done away with by deep penitence, or by works of satisfaction, e.g., prayers, alms, fastings, etc., or by patient endurance of troubles and adversities sent us by God, or by the satisfaction of our Lord Jesus Christ and the saints, applied to us by the church under certain conditions, which application we call an indulgence." "An indulgence is not, then, a pardon for sin; because sin must be remitted before an indulgence can be gained. Much less is it a permission to commit sin; for even God himself could not give such permission." "In order to gain any indulgence whatever, you must be in a state of grace." So say these deceivers; and we are told that it does not interest the masses of the community. To this we dissent. Nothing interests them more. We have waded through this long definition, not because there is any truth or honesty in it; but to show that, even if their statement is based on fact, Swinton's statement contains an acknowledged truth; and also to call attention to the truth, that an indulgence, as taught by Rome, is a stupendous lie, calculated to delude, and sure to damn the believer who trusts to this artifice. Indulgences had to do with sins to be committed. According to a book called "Tax of the Sacred Roman Chancery," in which are contained the exact sums to be levied for the pardon of each particular sin to be permitted, these are given:

s. d.

For procuring abortion — 7 6

"simony — 10 6

"sacrilege — 10 6

"taking a false oath in a criminal case — 90

"robbery — 120

"burning a neighbor's house — 120

"lying with a mother or sister — 76

"murdering a layman — 76

"defiling a virgin — 40

"keeping a concubine — 106

"laying violent hands on a clergyman — 106

In the light of such a statement, taken from Roman Catholic authorities, as much a fact as any other pricelist, Roman Catholics claim that an indulgence can only be granted in a state of grace. The fact is, indulgences cannot be granted at all. To say differently, is to belie the truth. Purgatory is only a delusion. Roman Catholic teaching controverts the truth. History simply shows that the Romish lie was born in 1096, that Urban II. was its inventor, and from that period deluded people have believed a lie that they might be damned. In 1300, Boniface issued an indulgence for all that would make a pilgrimage to Rome. A price was put on sins like shopkeepers' wares, and remission of sins by means of indulgences for jingling coin. The church, in 1517, was acting on the shameless principle of the Chamberlain of Innocent VIII. who said: "God willeth not the death of a sinner, but that he pay and live." In one of the pardon-tickets of 1517, there is a figure of a Domincan monk with a cross, crown of thorns, and a burning heart. In the upper corners is a nailed hand. On the front are the words:

"POPE LEO X. PRAYER.

"This is the length and breadth of the wounds of Christ in his holy side. As often as any one kisses it, he has seven years' indulgence." This has no reference to sins forgiven, and it is a lie to teach differently.

"The cross measured seven times makes the height of Christ in his humanity. He who kisses it is preserved for some days from sudden death, falling sickness, apoplexy."

The dealers put up the following notice: "The red indulgence-cross, with the pope's arms suspended on it, has the same virtue as the cross of Christ. The pardon makes those who accept it cleaner than baptism, purer even than Adam in a state of innocence in paradise. The dealer in pardons saves more people than Peter. The abuse went on until it became madness."*

Tetzel sold his indulgences to robbers, thieves and murderers, and claimed that they were as clean as Adam before his fall so soon as the click of the money was heard in the iron box. They tell the story of Tetzel and a robber. He bought an indulgence for a large sum, which gave him the privilege of committing any sin. The money went into the iron chest. Through a dark forest Tetzel and his chest were going. The robber stopped him, and demanded his money or his life. Tetzel told who he was. "I know you," said the robber, and pulled out the indulgence. Tetzel read. His sin had found him out. He lost his money; and the story proves the utter falsity of the claim that indulgences have only to do with sins remitted. This sin was to be committed.

Then came Luther. The Bible chained to the altar, had opened his eyes to the errors of Rome. Tossed by doubt, distressed by sin, he had gone to Rome: there he saw Romanism at its worst. The Bible in Erfurt library taught him another lesson than that of fasts and vigils. Luther now learned that a man was saved not by singing masses, but by the infinite grace of God. He said to the Pope fearlessly, as was his wont: "You are not God's vicegerent; you are another's, I think. I take your bull as an emparchmented lie, and burn it. You will do what you see good next; this is what I do." It was on the tenth of December, 1520, three years after the beginning of the business, that Luther, with a great concourse of people, took this indignant step of burning the Pope's

---

* Ludwig Hauser, p. 16.

decree in the market-place of Wittenberg. Wittenberg looked on with shoutings. The whole world was looking on. This was in 1520. In 1888, Boston is summoned to take up this work, and through remonstrance and argument kindle a fire which shall spread wider and rise higher, until it shall become unquenchable, and envelope all the world.

Say not that these questions of dogma should be left to theological disputants. They belong to the people. They influence life. They shape destiny.

HEAVEN OR HELL IS THE OUTCOME OF DOGMA.

Romanists deceive Romanists by statements which are false as to fact, and designed to be misleading as to inference. When they say, "that in order to gain any indulgence whatever, you must be in a state of grace," they make a declaration utterly wanting in truth. When Romanists talk about a state of grace they deceive. Romanism ignores a state of grace as Protestants understand it. The Bible teaches that a man passes into a state of grace when he is born again; when he is regenerated by the power of the Holy Ghost: then he becomes a new creature in Christ Jesus. Romanism ignores all this, and claims that an act of baptism, performed by a man, washes away sin. In other words, Romanism rests her hopes for salvation on baptismal regeneration and the sacraments.

The Word of God teaches, that "whoever confesses with the mouth the Lord Jesus, and believes in the heart that God raised him from the dead, he shall be saved." Rom. 10:9. When saved, he would not take an indulgence to sin were it offered to him; and would not use it if he had a million. He hates sin and loves holiness, when redeemed.

All this Luther saw, and learned that religion as it professed to be, and religion as it was embodied in the lives of church dignitaries, priests and friars, were in startling contrast. He knew his peril. John Huss had come to Rome with all imaginable promises and safe conducts. Rome turned her back on them all; they laid him instantly in a stone dungeon, three feet wide, six feet high, seven feet long, and burnt the true voice out of the world, choked it in smoke and fire. "The elegant pagan Leo

X., by this fire-decree," says Carlyle, "had kindled into noble, just wrath, the bravest heart then living in the world." Indulgences were farmed out to a bankrupt; in their sale, there was no more thought of religion than in the sale of lottery tickets.

Both lies are of the devil; and how a Congregational minister could forego the privilege of preaching the truth to the deceived, passes comprehension. He ignored his commission. He belied his profession, and betrayed his Lord. Either he knows better than to intimate that, for stating a truth, a book dealing with historic fact ought to be thrown out of the schools, and acts in this manner to curry favor with Romanists, and so ought to be retired from the School Board; or he does not know the truth, and is unfit for the position. In either event, the way out is his best way. The children need either a more honest, or a more intelligent man to represent their interests. This is not said in a spirit of raillery or pleasantry. We are dealing with momentous issues. God does not suffer us to trifle with the truth. " For it is impossible that those who were once enlightened, and have tasted of the heavenly gift, and were made partakers of the Holy Ghost, and have tasted the good Word of God, if they shall fall away, to renew them again unto repentance." (Heb. 6:4,5.)

Romanism deals with and in indulgences, in these days of Leo XIII., quite as much as it dealt with them in the days of Leo X. Romanism knows no improvement. Evolution theories may apply to science and to art, but not to Romanism. What Rome was in the dark ages, she is in this nineteenth century—as cruel, as blind, as selfish, as much opposed to education, as full of superstition as at any time in the past.

Sad and melancholy as is the truth, it is here, and evidently here to stay. There is a paper circulated among the young, called by a priestly name, which carries to the homes of vast numbers of individuals this fearful superstition and falsehood, known as indulgences, fresh from the hand of Leo XIII.

Here is an *Agnus Dei*, with a little of the earth from the foot of the cross, of which doubtless cartloads have been shipped away, which saves from drowning, etc. Here is a book bought at Donahue's, published in

Barclay street, New York, with the approbation of John Hughes, archbishop, as full of lies as an egg is full of meat, circulated among Romanists. This is the caption:

DEVOTION OF THE SCAPULARS.

Scapular of our Lady of Mount Carmel. "As it is considered a mark of distinction by men to have attendants wearing their livery, so does the Blessed Virgin like to see her servants wear her scapular; it should be a sign of their having devoted themselves to her service, and of their belonging to the family of the mother of God." (St. Alphonsus Liguori).

A scapular is a piece of cloth worn on the bosom, and on the back to procure indulgences to sin, or indulgences which shall free from the guilt or pain of sin. Now, Romanists are making a distinction between the payment of the debt in purgatory, and an indulgence to sin.

"And yet," said Archbishop Hughes, "we have spoken only of the scapular of our Blessed Lady of Mount Carmel. There are several others to which likewise many graces and indulgences are attached:

"1. *The Scapular of our Blessed Lady of the Seven Dolors,* of the Order of the Servants of Mary, founded in Florence, in 1133, by seven men, to whom the Blessed Virgin appeared, and commanded them to wear a black habit in memory of the Seven Dolors."

"2. *The Scapular of the Immaculate Conception of the Order of Theatines,* or Regular Clerks, which was founded by Peter John Caraffa, who was afterwards Pope, under the name of Paul IV., and died in the year 1559.

"3. *The Scapular of The Most Holy Trinity,* of the Order of Trinitarians, for the redemption of captives, which was founded in the twelfth century by St. John de Matha and St. Felix de Valois. These religious wear a white habit, with a cross of red and blue on the breast, as shown by an angel to St. John de Matha, and in which the Blessed Virgin appeared to St. Felix de Valois. These three Scapulars, like the Scapular of Mt. Carmel, are composed each of two small pieces of woolen cloth. When together with that of Mount Carmel, all four pieces square, or nearly so, are sewed together, like leaves of a book, and four more pieces exactly similar are sewed in like manner; then these two parts, four

199

pieces in each, are joined by two bands of tape about eighteen inches long, so that one part falls on the breast, and the other on the back, The largest piece is generally the Scapular of Mt. Carmel, which is of brown color; the second, which is somewhat smaller, is the Scapular of Our Lady of the Seven Dolors, and is of a black color; the third is, the Scapular of the Immaculate Conception, and is still smaller and of a blue color. This color, the emblem of resignation to Mary, was also the color of her mantle. The Scapular of the Most Holy Trinity is white, and the smallest of the four, in the middle of which there must be a cross, likewise of wool, one arm of which must be of red, the other blue. All these colors, as well as the cross, must be visible.

The Redemptorist Fathers have the power to give these three Scapulars. The essential requirement for all the indulgences and graces annexed to these three Scapulars is, to receive them from a priest empowered to grant them, and to wear them constantly. If any one loses or wears out the Scapular, he can take another in its stead. Those who, either though carelessness, or even through malice, neglect to wear it, or have laid it aside, can again resume it, and gain all the indulgences as before. The Scapular of the Most Holy Trinity alone is excepted; according to the declaration of Innocent XI., it must be blessed as often as renewed.

Indulgences are granted to those who wear the scapulars, by Paul V. in 1606, Clement X. in 1673, Clement XI. in 1710, Innocent XI. in 1680, '81, '82.

WHAT THEY CLAIM TO DO.

They teach that they save life. Proof: At the siege of Montpelier, in the year 1682, a soldier named M. deBeauregard, was struck by a musketball, which rested on the Scapular and saved his life. Louis XIII., King of France, saw it, and put on a Scapular. Monsieur de Cuge, cornet of a company of horse, was wounded at Tefin, in the year 1636, by a cannon ball, which, passing through the left side, tore his heart to pieces, so that, naturally, he could not live a moment. The Scapular saved him until the priest came; and so on, and so on.

If Romanists can do the one, they can do both. Besides, whenever indulgences are procured, the besotted run the risk, and plunge deeper into sin because of it.

To say, as does Rev. Dr, Duryea and the Boston School Board, that an indulgence is not a *permission to commit sin,* is to deceive the people. Said Tetzel: "Draw near, and I will give you letters duly sealed, *by which even the sins you shall hereafter desire to commit shall all be forgiven you. I* would not exchange my privileges for those of St. Peter in heaven; for I have saved more souls with my indulgences, than he with his sermons. There is no sin so great that the indulgence cannot reach it—let him pay largely, and it shall be forgiven him. *Even repentance is not indispensable."* Shall such facts be cast out of our school-books, that the generation now coming upon the stage of action may be surrendered to Rome?

In Canada is an indulgence of Pio Nono, offering to all who enlisted in his army indulgences for themselves and their relatives, framed and hung in the homes of the deluded. Here is one that offers 100 days' indulgence each time repeated, signed Pius IX., 3d June, 1874. Here is another offering indulgences to all who will contribute to the building of the University College of Ottawa: the holder of this certificate shall be entitled to share twenty-five masses daily, and in all the prayers and good works of the Rev. Oblate Fathers,

For ten years, by a contribution of — 25 cents.

Forever — $200

A family, for ten years — $100

Thus are men and women deceived. They trust in man, rather than in the efficacy of the atonement by Jesus Christ. This gives them power at sickbeds over the wills of the dying, and over the purses of living relatives and friends. From the living they get profit in the sale of indulgences, *Agnus Deis,* scapularies, masses of every kind, dispensations from fasts, removal of impediments to marriage, miraculous medals, various defences against the devil, grace through the images or relics of patron saints, and other similar devices.

Remember, there is nothing to be gotten from the Roman Catholic church without money. No money, no baptism; no money, no marriage; no money, no burial; no money, nothing.

If Romanists deceive Romanists, it becomes Christians to preach to them the gospel. The mortification and shame which came to us because of one who professes allegiance to Christ, is very hard to bear. Let the shame and disgrace end there. Christians, awake, and put your armor on! Napoleon in Egypt, close by the pyramids, said: "Twenty centuries behold your actions." Christian people, look up to the throne. Jesus is there. Look about you, behold the perishing.

Romanists are crowding the broad road to death. Millions of youth are interested in this controversy. Will Americans rise to the level of their great opportunity and do their whole duty? or will they bow down to Rome, and barter away their God-given rights? This is the question of the hour! How will it be answered? Shall men be taught error, or the truth? Remember, "as a man thinketh in his heart, so is he." Think right, and all will be well. Think wrong and act wrong, and ruin awaits you.

17

Can Washington be Taken Out of the Lap of Rome

THIS MAY YET COME TO the question of the hour. If done, it must be accomplished through the combined efforts of the people of the United States. The North and the South, the East and the West, must come up alike to the help of the Lord against the mighty. The need of it is apparent. It is the boast of the Frenchman, that as goes Paris, so goes France. As went Rome, so went Italy. And so it may yet be said, As goes Washington, so will go the great Republic.

Remember, France made Paris bend her neck to the people. Italy thundered at the gates of Rome; took away the States of the Church from His Holiness the Pope; tossed overboard, with contempt and ease, the ruler who was said to preserve the *equipoise* of Europe; sent him a prisoner to the Vatican; and went on with the work of making Italy free, as if the tap-root of Papal Rule had not been the growth of centuries. Washington, the centre of political influence and activity, is in the lap of Rome, with the consent of the people. Let there be a protest. Unroof the monster, Jesuitism. Uncover the pollution, the scandal of the confessional. Unlock and throw open the doors of the convents and nunneries, the assignation houses, kept for a so-called celibate priesthood. Expose the conduct of those who have made prostitution flourish at Rome and in all the great cities in which they have control, and Washington will shake off the incubus. The nation will declare for purity, for justice, for emancipation from the shackles of blind and besotted Romanism, and from the thraldom of the black-robed throng, who insult their sick, half-starve their orphans,—for whose support they are paid by the State,—and maltreat their poor; because in the heart of Rome love is exchanged for selfish greed. Not always will statesmen bow and cringe to obtain the Roman Catholic vote, which is only powerful because it is always on sale, going to the highest bidder, without regard to principle. It will yet appear that fifty millions of people, blessed with liberty, and in the presence of wonderful opportunity, cannot afford to creep under the black wing of Papal despotism, that vampire that sucked the lifeblood out of Spain, out of Mexico, and out of any country where it has been permitted to do its hellish work undisturbed. Christianity is the product of witnessing for the truth. The Papacy is the monument of withholding testimony for God. Error is the servant of the "Prince of the power of the air." Truth is the helpmeet of God. Witnessing for the truth is to result in the overthrow of every form of error. There are reasons for this faith. Let us enumerate a few of them:

1. *God is for the truth.* When we say that, the argument assures the people of victory so soon as they are made ready to stand with and for God. By grace, by Providence, by the help of God's true children, in uncounted and in unexpected ways, aid will be brought to those who put on the whole armor of God and stand ready to fight the good fight of faith. The achievements wrought by truth, and for the truth, in other days and on other fields, attest the truth that God works for those who work for him.

DARK DATS THERE HAVE BEEN.

Here is an illustration. Death, the fire, and the inquisitorial torture of Romish hate, had achieved an apparent victory. The night was dark, because the witnesses were still.

In 1514 the Council met in Rome. Into the Market Place strode a servant of the Church of Rome, and in pride asked, "Is there one who protests?" He waited. He listened. The Waldensians were dead in France. In England the Lollards were exterminated. In Italy truth had been slain in the street. *"Not one protests!"* It was a terrible charge brought by Rome against Rome. Thousands and tens of thousands passed from the Cross to the stake. They were burned, tortured, hurled over rocks. Rome reveled in barbarity.

"The rack, the fagot, or the hated creed Were the tender mercies of tyrant Home;

While, fearless amidst Christ's fold fierce wolves did roam, And stainless sheep upon her altars bleed."

In May 1514, the testimony ceased. Three years and a half pass. It is a prophetic period. Look! Up the stair-way climbs Martin Luther on his knees. Hark! A voice sounds down to him. He is tired, sick, hopeless, despondent, a type of all Romanists. "The just shall live by faith," passes through the gateway of the conscience to the chamber of the soul. It startles him. It unlocks night. It uncovers the crucified Christ. Clouds depart. He is born again. He is in a new world. He confesses it. He becomes a witness. God helps his own. Everything is made ready for the work. The banner is unfurled. Redeemed men take it and bear it on. The friends of error are powerless, in presence of the testimony of living and brave witnesses.

Think how Zwingle, Luther, Melancthon, William, Prince of Orange, told the truth! They carried their testimony into towns, into churches, and into homes. They told what God did for them. As justification by faith placed them on vantage ground, they called to men in night and gloom to come to the light, and held up to them the reeking cross, which broke the power of "the man of sin " and gave deliverance to captive souls.

TRUTH DISINTEGRATES ROMANISM.

Romanism was born, and found its place of being and its capacity of growth, because of the surrender of the individual conscience to the keeping of a machine.

Every effort put forth by the individual in behalf of the truth is a subtraction from the power which upholds the Papacy, and an addition to the power which is to people the world with hope, and make the desert to bud and blossom as the rose. Hence every movement in favor of individual thinking favors Christianity and opposes Romanism. Every scintillation of truth in behalf of freedom, every word spoken for God and the right, clears the way for humanity, and widens the area of the kingdom of God. There is nothing in Romanism calculated to charm or please the thinking and unfettered intellect. It stultifies reason where it can; it banishes God's word as best it may; that word which is the foundation of the World's jurisprudence, the fountain-source of liberty, and the pillar of flame and cloud, by whose aid the nation has made its march out of the wilderness of trial into the Canaan of possession. Romanism fetters the mind, enslaves the limb, and is the servant of injustice, the parent and source of despotism, and the foe of all that ennobles and exalts humanity. This is coming to be known and felt. Romanists are feeling it quite as much as others. Christ is leading on.

"He has sounded forth the trumpet that shall never call retreat;
He is sifting out the hearts of men before His judgment seat;
O be swift my soul to answer Him I be jubilant my feet!
Our God is marching on.

"In the beauty of the lilies, Christ was born, across the sea,—
With a glory in his bosom that transfuses you and me.
As he died to make men holy, let us die to make men
free,—While God is marching on."

Somebody will catch this inspiration, and become the trumpeter of a great truth. Some one will appear, not only as the scourge of impositions, and the ponderous hammer that shall smite upon the brazen idolatry of the age, but as the upbuilder of holy principles in accordance with the teachings of the Word of God.

It is essential that a clear conception be obtained of the work *to be done.*

A free Church in a free State was once the battle cry of the Republic. Rome is organizing an aggressive warfare upon the separation of Church and State. It was the hope of promoting a union of Church and State that made the Red-Robed Cardinal desire the company of a son of a Presbyterian minister, occupying the position of President, in laying the cornerstone of the Jesuit college. It is to be proclaimed that the religion of Jesus Christ is to be divorced from the State. This is not because Republicans honor religion less. They believe that the Church of Christ is a divine institution, which has to do with finding out the truth, holding the truth, and spreading the truth.

They believe also in the State; claim that it is also a divine institution, and has sacred duties, such as guaranteeing to every man safety, and making his person, his property, and his right to think and be. The State must be *safety, justice, righteousness.* There must be a free Church in a free State, the State subject to justice only, the Church subject to Christ only.

True Americans must see that the very antipodes of the idea just stated is the Romish idea. Rome claims that the Church shall be all, and the State a non-entity, and that the Roman Catholic religion shall be permitted to exclude all other forms of faith. The Pope declares, that it is an error to be reprobated and proscribed, that the Church shall be separate from the State. Americans are to take note of this, and be made ready to antagonize it.

Rome claims that it is "an error to be reprobated, proscribed, and condemned, to say that, in the case of conflicting laws between the two powers, the civil law ought to prevail, and that the church has not the power of availing herself of force, or any direct or indirect temporal power." These propositions—so clear, so startling—bear date Dec. 4th, 1864, of "Errors Condemned," and were reaffirmed by the late Plenary Council of Baltimore. Truly has it been said: "There is enough dynamite in these propositions to blow up our entire modern civilization, destroy liberty of conscience, and bring utter ruin upon the purity of the church and the integrity of the State."

Americans know that in the United States, at the present time, there is a union of Church and State to an extent little dreamed of.

In New Jersey, the State Reform School has been Romanized. The unsectarian teaching, in piety and morals, has been destroyed. The moral and religious training of the Catholic boys is handed over completely to the Romish Church. The same is true of the City of New York, where children arrested are given over to institutions under the control of the religion professed by their parents. As a result, there are 3,000 Roman

Catholic youth in the New York Protectory, more lost to Protestantism than if they were born and reared in Rome.

The State thus gives a guarantee to the Roman Catholic Church, that no child of Romish parents shall be permitted to come in contact with the free thought of our American life and with the religion of our Lord Jesus Christ. This is not liberty of conscience; this is coercion of conscience. The American people will see this; and seeing it, they will correct the legislation that makes it live and thrive under the shadow of the broad *Aegis* of our Republic.

Again: Rome seeks to take the children of the State out of the control of the civil power. This is the exact language of the Syllabus: That" the entire direction of public schools in which the youth of Christian States are educated, may and must appertain to the civil power, is an error to be reprobated and proscribed. Issue must here be joined."

We want in our land no fractional parts of Americans—we want whole men, who are rooted in American ideas. The Baltimore Plenary Council decided, that all Catholic children shall be educated in parochial schools. This education will give us mutilated men and women. The American people must be made to see this, and they will resist the encroachment.

"I wonder," said Dr. Dollinger of Germany, the Old Catholic, who fought the conferring of the decree of Infallibility upon Pio Nono,—"I wonder if they understand in America what an infallible Pope means? that it means a hand stretched over into the United States, and laid upon every Roman Catholic citizen, and imposing upon him the obligation to set himself up in opposition to the ordinances of your Government whenever the Pope shall pronounce his judgments against these ordinances on moral or religious ground?" Yes, Dr. Dollinger, a great many understand it, and are getting ready to deliver Roman Catholics from their thraldom.

Roman Catholics are getting more money for the support of Romish schools than is given to all the Evangelical churches combined. The New York *Independent* affirms, that Protestant schools find more difficulty in getting what they ask for than the Romish schools. It affirms that Government interferes less with Romish schools than with Protestant. It affirms that, in the schools wholly supported by the Government, they are rapidly passing into the control of the Roman Catholics, even where all are Protestants, as among the Indians.

A Roman Catholic was kept at the head of the postal service until it was very largely Romanized, with Roman Catholics for postmasters wherever they could be pushed in; and then he was transferred to the Interior Department to Romanize that; while the head of the army, a Roman Catholic, gave a Roman Catholic sutler control of every army post, and the nation donates, even against fundamental law, a lot of land at every military post, on which to build a Roman Catholic chapel.

The American people only need to be made acquainted with these facts, and they will antagonize them.

Our fathers clamored for a separation of Church and State. Let their children go on with the work. It has been well said: "If we work to serve the twentieth century, we must save the *nineteenth.*" We must reconstruct our geography, and permit the Tiber to flow into the Potomac, and not compel the Potomac to flow into the Tiber.

Create a literature that shall point out the vices and corruptions of Romanism.

Popery must be antagonized; Christ must be championed. This, politicians will come to see. They will insist upon a separation of Church and State; upon maintaining a public school system, in which all the children of the State *shall* be educated. The Bible shall be unbound. This made way for Luther, so that when he came they breathed an air which had long been most patiently impregnated with the very essence of innovation. The word of God in the hands of the people is the accusing spirit of the Papacy. In the days of Wicliff, "*the noise of its wings*" were faintly heard in England.

Then, men of position, indignant at the impoverishment and disgrace of their country, antagonized the power of Rome. Afterwards men fought it, because of the perversion and abuse of their religious institutions. Hence, when the conflict under Luther began, the leader of it could number potentates among his allies and partizans, till, at last, he may be said to have had

> "A kingdom for a stage, princes for actors,
> And monarchs to behold the swelling scene."

Not so at the present time. Our great men seem to be our greatest cowards.

In pulpits, in pressrooms, and on platforms, it is fashionable to be servile. What kings did in Europe who held the stirrup for His Holiness to mount, that presidents and politicians in free America seem ready to do. It is not in our stars, but in ourselves, that we are underlings to Rome. The Church of Rome is being pandered to by men who will ere long wake up to their shame. What mean these "Roman Catholic Notes" that meet the approval of Roman Catholic officials, except as an indication that the Roman Catholic vote is a thing that may be bargained for. How humiliating the fact! Seven millions of men and women in free America for sale to the highest bidder! For that vote, politicians betray God, turn their backs upon liberty, surrender the dearest rights of freemen to the keeping of their bitterest foe. A distinguished statesman goes to Rome; enters the American College, so-called,—in fact, a college built by Americans to change American youth into Italian priests; there he referred to the Church of Rome as "that Church which is so widely spread and so profoundly respected." Where is it "respected" by any one? Had he *said, feared,* by all in America, and by himself more than all, he had told the truth.

To stand up against Rome at this hour requires high courage. Thousands have it. Millions will yet possess it.

2. *God* is *against Romanism.* Prophecy declares it. History brings proof in support of the proposition; and from no nation so truly as from the story of the life of the Republic of the United States. Romanism is disintegrating, wherever the truth concerning it is told. It resembles an ice-glacier loosened from its Northern home. The current bears it southward. The gulf-stream of liberty catches it and dissolves it.

Superstition is being scattered broadcast by the brightness of the Sun of Righteousness.

The overthrow of the Papacy is simply the unfulfilled prophecy of that Being who described its coming and its doom. The same Eye that saw the rise and decline of Mohammedanism,—the same Being who gave the command, "Loose the four angels which are bound in the great river Euphrates," (Rev. 9 :14), before the Islam horsemen swept forth in their career of conquest; and that commanded the sixth angel to pour out his vial upon the great river Euphrates when the water was dried up (Rev. 16: 12), and the way was prepared for the kings who are from the rising of the sun, so that Turkey is destroyed, and is a captive enslaved, the sport and plaything of Continental powers; that foretold the settlement of America when he pointed to the ships of Tarshish on their way to the land of broad rivers,— described the character and the occupation of the "beast " of prophecy, and portrayed the "woman" clothed in purple and scarlet and holding in her hand the cup of her fornications and upon her head the writing: *"Mystery! Babylon the great! The Mother of Harlots and of the abominations of the earth."* This the people begin to see. Sound the battle-cry.

THE WORK IS ONLY BEGUN.

The possibility of bearing witness for Christ is within reach of all. It is possible to carry truth within the citadel of the enemy, through the agency of the help employed in our houses and in our places of business.

Never do I think of the millions about us, who want something better than these mummeries to satisfy the cravings of their immortal souls, but I rejoice that the Gospel, as we know it, is the power of God and the wisdom of God, suited to their every need. Tell them of it. There is no mistaking what it will do for them. It will save their souls, and give them a joy and peace they seek elsewhere in vain.

The Holy Spirit works for those who work for God. There are links in the chain of God's providence which enter into the chain that is mighty to the pulling down of the stronghold of error. Children of God,

211

be true. Things of deep interest are pending. Let soul touch soul. Let truth combat error; and the people of the Lord, beautiful as Tirzah, comely as Jerusalem, shall be terrible as an army with banners!

The Lord Jehovah reigneth. Let the people rejoice. For from God we obtain the assurance that witnessing for the truth shall result in the taking of Washington out of the lap of Rome, making her the glory of the Nation, and the Light-house of the World; so that the millions now shrouded in darkness shall awake to the touch of the new-born radiance, and leaving their idols behind, shall walk forth into the new day—heirs of God, and joint-heirs with Jesus Christ, to an inheritance incorruptible, and undefiled, and that fadeth not away. AMEN AND AMEN.